Home at Last

Bonne Fête
Christine !

Ton Oncle

Wilfrid

EDITED BY ROSALIND MOSS

# Home At Last

CATHOLIC ANSWERS
SAN DIEGO
2000

Published by Catholic Answers, Inc.
2020 Gillespie Way
El Cajon, California 92020
(888) 291-8000 (orders)
(619) 387-0042 (fax)
www.catholic.com (Web)
Cover design by Laurie Miller
Printed in the United States of America
ISBN 1-888992-20-4

# With Thanksgiving

I will be eternally grateful to Mitch and Zhava Glaser and to John MacArthur who led me to the Lamb of God twenty-four years ago and who mentored me through my Evangelical years. And to Scott Hahn, Karl Keating, Msgr. James T. O'Connor, Fr. Peter Vianney, Ronda Chervin, and, above all, to my beloved brother, David, for leading me all the way home to the Lamb's Church in all its fullness.

I give special thanks also to Trask Tapperson for his gracious assistance throughout this project and to my friend and neighbor, Sharon Junion, for her keen ear and devoted heart.

And thanks upon thanks to my fellow pilgrims whose stories lie herein, who have traveled the path to Rome, not without cost, and who have found it, as have I, the pearl of great price, worth selling everything for.

May their journeys be an encouragement to all who enter in and give honor to the One to whom all glory is due.

# Table of Contents

# Preface

Recently I was at a conference on Catholic evangelization at Franciscan University of Steubenville. While browsing in the university's bookstore I met a man and his wife who were also attending the conference. To my surprise they told me that they were both ministers in the Assembly of God.

"What are two Protestant ministers doing at a Catholic conference on evangelization?" I asked. The wife said that both of them, after much study and prayer, had decided some time ago to find out more about the Catholic Church. And they told me, smiling, that they were to be received into the Church two weeks after the conference. Taking this step, they said, had required many sacrifices, because they loved their ministry and they loved the congregation that they had been serving.

I had to know: "What was it that drew you to the Church?" They replied, "It was the Eucharist—we hunger for the body and blood of Jesus Christ."

They had found that the Catholic Church took seriously the words of Jesus about being the bread of life. They had grasped that the accounts of the Last Supper clearly indicate that our Lord was talking, not about a symbol, but about the bread and wine truly becoming his body and blood.

The couple recounted how surprised they had been to find that the Church, far from being disconnected from Scripture, has scriptural bases for the sacraments and for other major elements of Catholic life. They knew their Bible well, and they had come to the conclusion that the Catholic Church truly was the most biblical Christian church, the one must deeply rooted in the Scriptures. Furthermore, they had become convinced that to be a

Christian means to be united to the successor of Peter, and they found that only the Catholic Church could offer that union.

As we conversed, they also shared with me their observation that many times "cradle Catholics" seem to take the Eucharist, the papacy, and many other elements of the Church for granted, whereas those who must struggle to find and to accept the Catholic faith seem to appreciate the richness of the Church in a special way.

This interesting couple is not unique. In many ways, in fact, their story is familiar. For today there are many non-Catholics, from people of no faith to people of profound faith—indeed, even Protestant ministers like these—who are being drawn to the Catholic Church.

Why?

The modern world has much to offer, but there is a hunger in the soul that it cannot nourish. In this country we have the highest standard of living we've ever known. We have forms of medical diagnosis, intervention, and repair that are well-nigh miraculous. We have sophisticated systems of communications and information distribution. And we have endless entertainment available at the push of a button.

But amid all these developments, we feel a spiritual hunger that none of these can satisfy. God has placed in each of us a desire to know and to love him. The security-seeking and pleasure-loving culture we have developed cannot answer that desire, and in fact does its best to encourage us to ignore our hunger for the living God. Our culture has complacently dubbed itself "post-Christian," but "neo-pagan," in the the minds of many Christians, might be a more apt description.

Many mainline Protestant churches have caved into the neo-pagan culture, watering down previously held doctrines about the divinity of Jesus and the centrality of God, and abandoning positions on abortion, marriage, and sexuality. Churches should be in tension with the prevailing culture. If a church is not, then it becomes irrelevant and meaningless.

Despite the collapse of spiritual and moral values in our nation, the Catholic Church has remained steadfast in teaching right and wrong and in reclaiming the values of Jesus. And people who feel that there must be more to life than what the surrounding culture can offer are hearing the Church's voice.

Particularly open to hearing that voice are people who have committed themselves to seeking the truth in faithful adherence to Scripture and Tradition. The clear teaching and loving welcome of the Catholic faith draw such people in, and they are becoming Catholic because they see that the Catholic Church, and only the Catholic Church, contains the fullness of the teaching that Jesus and the apostles intended for the Church.

The spiritual hunger of which I speak cannot be satisfied with slim rations. It must be offered the full plate of Christianity. Protestant churches and some Fundamentalist sects certainly offer important nourishment through their devotion to Christ and the Scriptures. What they do not and cannot offer are certain truths of the faith that have stood unchanged for 2,000 years:

- The Mass, which is what former Catholics miss most;

- The great blessing of the Eucharist, mentioned in the Bible and instituted by Jesus Christ;

- The Magisterium, the Church's teaching authority, expressed through the Holy Father and the bishops who are successors to Peter and the apostles. With them there is a way to know what the teachings of the Church are;

- Mary and the knowledge that Christian revelation is incomplete unless there is a place for the mother of Jesus, who is mentioned as being present at critical moments in the life of her Son;

- Tradition, the distillation of the riches of the Church's living heritage of two thousand years, and,

- Great teachings on social justice, proclaiming respect for the dignity of each human person. Through them the Church speaks often, and eloquently, about the dignity of all human life, even when the bearer of that life is sick or elderly or yet unborn.

This is the full menu of Christianity. This is the wholeness and integrity which drew the converts who tell their stories in this delightful and substantial book.

These people speak of their sense that, in coming to the "one, holy, catholic, and apostolic church," they have come home. It is a feeling that I think I understand. I think of the impressive Bernini colonnade that encloses St. Peter's Square in Rome. The double rows of columns that stretch out from both sides of St. Peter's Basilica have been described as the arms of the Church reaching out to welcome all peoples, all language groups, all cultures—to gather in all individuals looking for truth and wishing to find happiness in this life and eternal salvation in the next.

Our beloved converts have come home to the Church as children to the arms of a loving mother. They prayed, argued, studied, wondered. And finally they embraced, and were embraced by, the Catholic faith. It wasn't by their works alone that they found a home in the Church. Ultimately they, like all Catholics, are members of the Church because of God's generous gift of faith, a gift that we neither earn nor deserve.

May the converts in this book, and all like them, persevere in their newfound faith and bear fruit a hundredfold.

—Most Reverend Michael J. Sheehan,
Archbishop, Diocese of Santa Fe

*Most Reverend Michael J. Sheehan became Archbishop of Santa Fe, New Mexico, in 1993 after serving for ten years as the first bishop of Lubbock, Texas. He is the former chairman of the Evangelization Committee of the National Conference of Catholic Bishops.*

# Foreword

In recent years there have appeared many collections of "convert stories," accounts of how individuals were led by the Holy Spirit into full communion with the Catholic Church. In earlier times, these would have been called "confessions." Now here is another volume describing the spiritual pilgrimages of Catholic converts.

Why publish more of these "confessions"?

Two reasons. The first is this: Though the destination—Rome—is always the same, each convert travels a unique road to reach that home. Each story, therefore, offers Catholics a new viewpoint and a fresh look at the Church they sometimes take for granted. Furthermore, each story offers non-Catholic readers an invitation to take up the search for truth that can lead them also into Catholic communion. Many Catholic converts have told me that reading about others who have come home to the Catholic Church greatly helped them to recognize and accept the truth of Catholicism.

A person changes from one religious tradition (or no recognizable tradition) to another for one of two reasons. Either he likes the new religion for some reason and therefore thinks it must be true, or he realizes that it is true and that he must embrace it whether he likes it or not. The former approach is subjective and emotional; the latter, objective and intellectual.

The subjective approach is well illustrated in the advice that two of our contributors received from well-meaning friends. Their friends told these seekers they would never find a church that exactly suited them. Give up the search, they said. Instead, the seekers should find a church where they felt comfortable, where they liked the people, where they basically agreed with what was being taught. The issue of truth was not raised. One might call it a "shopping" mentality. One who shops for a church home despairs of ever finding the truth; that is, if he ever consciously sought it.

One sees this attitude in a book published several years ago that described the process by which half a dozen or so Roman Catholics decided to become Episcopalians. Neither the word "truth" nor anything like it appears in the book. There is not a single reference to Scripture. All the reasons given are purely subjective: I did not like this or that about Catholicism, and I liked this or that in the Episcopal church. Significantly, some of these converts to the Episcopal church openly admitted that they wanted to be in a church where there was "more ambiguity" on moral matters (by which they meant sexual morality).

In contrast, all the converts whose stories you will read in this book took an objective approach to seeking their church home. Though various subjective factors entered into their seeking, all came to realize that the truth of Jesus, the whole truth of the gospel, can be found only within the Church which he founded. They had already come to know and love the Savior. Now they knew they must love him not on their terms (which was all they had as Protestants or as pagans) but on his terms. They could do this only by submitting to Christ in a new way: Christ speaking to them through his Church.

For most, the journey was not easy. These converts learned well the truth of our Lord's words, "Do not think that I have come to bring peace on earth; I have not come to bring peace, but a sword" (Matt. 10:34). Despite opposition and bitter criticism and even ostracism from friends and family, they resolutely followed the prompting of the Holy Spirit. In speaking of the difficulties they encountered on their pilgrimage, these converts are not complaining; they are simply reporting. The promise of Jesus unfolded in their lives in mysterious ways: "You will know the truth, and the truth will make you free" (John 8:32).

These new Catholics safely reached and now gratefully live in their true home because they came for the right reason. One can think of many possible reasons for a non-Catholic to enter the

Church. None of them in itself, perhaps, might be wrong. But apart from the right reason, "none, finally," will bring a peaceful, joyful life within the Church.

After Vatican II, the first married man ordained to the permanent diaconate in this country (and perhaps in the world) was formerly a Church of England minister. He received much publicity in the Catholic press simply because he was the first permanent deacon. A year after he was ordained, he announced that he and his wife were returning to the Church of England. The reason he gave was this: He had become a Catholic because he had believed the Catholic Church was the best vehicle for proclaiming the gospel today. In his year in the Church he had decided otherwise. That was why he was resuming his membership in the Church of England.

Assuming that the man truly spoke his reason for leaving the Church, one can readily see that he came into the Church for the wrong reason. He became a Catholic because of a subjective evaluation of the Church: "I can use that structure for my ministry," so to speak. He never really became a Catholic; he never submitted himself to Jesus Christ speaking through his one Church. To speak of the man's relationship to the Church in marital terms, that marriage was invalid from the outset.

The converts whose stories are given here all came in for the right reason. That is, they realized that what the Catholic Church teaches about herself is true. They realized, some after long years of seeking and studying and praying, that she is the one true Church established by Jesus Christ. They realized that she alone has been entrusted with the fullness of truth and the means of grace. They realized that she has been authorized by Christ to speak in his name and with his authority.

And there's more. They realized that once they came to know the truth about the Church, they had no alternative but to act on that truth. They would never again be the same. They could not remain outside her communion, deceiving themselves—as Anglo-Catholics do—by thinking that because they agreed with her teaching they were in fact Catholics. In the *Dogmatic Constitution of the Church,* Vatican II warned against this thinking. To paraphrase the Council's teaching, anyone who knows what the Catholic Church is, knows the truth of what she teaches about herself. Anyone who comes to this knowledge and refuses either to enter her or, once within, to remain in her communion, "cannot be saved." The reason is, that person would be rejecting Jesus Christ himself.

Coming into the Church for the right reason enabled these converts to see through the human problems in the Church and not to be distracted or perhaps repelled by them. Being loyal to the Holy Father and to the Church's teaching, they understand and deplore the confusion created by rebellious Catholics. Unlike the dissenters, the converts have no desire to redefine the Catholic faith according to their own tastes. One converted clergyman who had encountered great hardships in his journey said in my hearing, "My wife and I have gone through hell to get here. We're not about to start being Protestant all over again in the Catholic Church. We're with the *Pope!*"

Occasionally non-Catholic friends remind us that traffic flows out of the Catholic Church as well as into it. It is true that the traffic is two-way, but the two streams are quite different. Judging from the experience of many other converts, and from my contacts with large numbers of converts through the Coming Home Network, I offer a challenge to non-Catholics who speak of traffic out of, as well as into, the Church.

The challenge is this: Show me one Catholic who really understood and devotedly practiced the Catholic faith; a Catholic who loved the Church; a Catholic who, through serious study and reflection and prayer concluded that the Episcopal church (or Presbyterian or Methodist or other denomination) is in fact the one true Church established by Christ; a Catholic who concluded that that particular church, speaking with one voice, is the appointed representative of Christ on earth. Out of the group of nominal Catholics leaving the Church for other traditions, show me one Catholic who fits this description.

There is nothing daring about this challenge. It is safe, because there are no takers. Catholics who leave the Church for one of the denominations never make their decision for the reasons just given. The reasons are always subjective: dislike of something the Catholic Church teaches; resentment over treatment received from some Catholic (perhaps a priest or a religious); the attraction of small, friendly congregations; and above all, the determination to decide for oneself what is true Christianity.

Read the exciting stories these new Catholics have to tell. Rejoice with them that they have come fully into the Mystical Body of Christ. And pray that countless others outside the Church's communion will follow these courageous examples.

—Fr. Ray Ryland

*Fr. Ryland, a former Episcopal clergyman, is adjunct professor of theology at Franciscan University of Steubenville, chaplain of the Coming Home Network, and assistant pastor at Holy Family Church in Steubenville. He lives with his wife, Ruth, in Steubenville, Ohio.*

# Introduction

What makes a soul long for God? What is it that stirs the heart so that all the world cannot satisfy it? Why are some content to travel through life without ever asking where we came from or where we're going, while others feel keenly their need for meaning, for purpose, for wholeness? And what would cause some, having found meaning, having found the truth of God in Christ, to venture beyond their initial discovery to find the Church he established on earth?

Years ago, I took a job at a halfway house for troubled teens. After several weeks, I was fired for having spoken to those young distraught women about the God I had come to know. Not long after, I received a call from one of the teens telling me that Kathy, a seventeen-year-old with whom I had spent nights in the hospital because of her drug overdoses and epileptic seizures, had gone down onto Hollywood Boulevard and put a gun to her head. She was dead.

"Why?" I asked. Why me? Why did God save *me*? Why not Kathy? I was no more worthy than she.

Years later, as I entered the Catholic Church, believing it to be the fullness of all God has given on earth, I asked again, "Why me?" Why not John MacArthur, J. I. Packer, R. C. Sproul—pastors, teachers, mentors who taught me to love truth, people to whom I will be eternally grateful? Why not a thousand people worthier and certainly more intelligent than I? Why has God poured out such grace on me to cause me to search further? I don't know the answer. I know only that salvation, from beginning to end, is all of grace. And the paths of God's leading are as varied as the multitudes that have found their way home.

I'll never tire of the stories of pilgrims from every walk of life and faith who have traveled the path to Rome—to the Church our Savior promised to build, to lead into all truth, and to be with until the end of time. Nor do I imagine I'll ever get used to the fact that I'm in that Church, the Church that is home.

I recall a beloved song from my Evangelical years:

> *This world is not my home,*
> *I'm just a-passin' through.*
> *My treasures are laid up*
> *Somewhere beyond the blue.*
> *The angels beckon me*
> *From heaven's open door,*
> *And I can't feel at home*
> *In this world anymore.*

There's a sense in which this world has never been my home. All my years I longed for something more. It was a longing, I now know, for what *should* be. It should be that we are incomplete apart from knowing the one who loved us and gave himself for us. "And this is eternal life," said our Lord, "that they know thee the only true God, and Jesus Christ whom thou hast sent" (John 17:3).

I came to know him through the only form of Christianity I had encountered and had come to trust, as a child trusts the earthly home into which he is born. I soon was faced, however, with the fact that the family of God into which I was reborn was split into thousands of denominations, each claiming the truth of the "pure and simple gospel."

"Does it matter?" some would ask. "Does it matter what one believes, or where one worships, as long as one believes in God?"

"Of course it matters," I would answer. That was obvious. "It's the *truth*, Jesus said, that sets us free."

"How do we come to know truth?"

"Through the Word of God, the Bible."

"But thousands of godly pastors and teachers come to as many conclusions about what the Scriptures mean by what they say."

"I know. It's not what should be. But in our fallen state we 'see through a glass darkly.' We do the best we can this side of heaven. One day we'll know as we are known."

What else could one answer? Division in doctrine and practice even among churches that were somewhat like-minded was a reality one needed to accept. But eighteen years of immersion in such a divided Christianity, even within the Evangelical camp, served only to increase the grief of my heart at the utter confusion being presented to a lost world—and to the sheep within what was supposed to be one fold with one Shepherd.

The question was once posed to me, "Suppose Christ had truly established a church, and suppose, in doing so, he left a teaching authority on earth in order that we might know, with certainty, what he meant by what he said. Would you want to know that?"

"Of course I would want to know. The question is, Did he do that?"

And how can we know? One clue is to take seriously the apostle Paul's words, which apply to the history of ancient Israel as truly as they apply to us today: "'What no eye has seen, nor ear heard, nor the heart of man conceived, what God has prepared for those who love him,' God has revealed to us through the Spirit" (1 Cor. 2:9-10).

For 2,000 years before Christ, God formed a people for his name from Abraham on. They were a *qahal* (in Hebrew), an assembly, a convocation, a community, a family, a people set apart. They were a spiritual community with God as their Father. And they were also a visible community that could be identified by their government, their worship, their liturgy, their dress, their food, their customs, by what they did and did not do. They were set apart by God, not to be isolated from the world but to be a light to the pagan peoples around them, to lead the nations to the one true God.

It was absolutely foreign to their thinking that any one individual or group would do its own thing, that anyone would decide how he would worship or interpret the Law for himself. And if anyone did (as in the case of Aaron's sons), he would be put to death.

God revealed himself as holy and taught his people that they were to imitate him in holiness. They were to be an obedient, worshipping, faithful people—not because God is a tyrant, but because he is a God of great love, a father who knows how to care for his children and bring them, through the means he provides, to their full happiness.

And he gave his people Israel a mission, a calling, a vocation: to bear witness to the Messiah to come. And come he did, in the fullness of time, to seek and to save the lost and to give his life as a ransom for many. Jesus came, not to do away with Israel of old, but so that the gospel would be taken to the four corners of the earth and that the people of God would be gathered from every tribe and tongue and nation. Jesus Christ is God, the same yesterday, to-day, and forever. As he formed Israel of old, he has formed for himself a *new* covenant people for his name.

Gathered with his disciples at the Sea of Galilee, Jesus said to Peter, "You are Peter and upon this rock I will build my church." The word Jesus used for church, *ekklesia*, is the Greek translation of the Hebrew word *qahal*. We are the new Israel, the spiritual Israel, the people of God, the new *qahal*, the *ekklesia*, the called-out ones. The Church, like Israel of old, can be identified by a visible unity, by God-given leadership, worship, and beliefs—she is a city set on a hill that cannot be hidden.

We are the very dwelling place of God—not as individuals only, but as his Body, the Church, the very household of God (1 Tim. 3:15). "There is one body," wrote the apostle Paul, "and one Spirit . . . one hope . . . one Lord, one faith, one baptism, one God and Father of us all, who is above all and through all and in all" (Eph. 4:4-6). It is he who has promised to lead his Church into all truth (John 16:13) and to be with it until the end of time (Matt. 28:20).

The night before Jesus was nailed to the cross for our sins, he spoke to his Father of the deepest desire of his heart: that we would be one as he and the Father are one.

I have manifested thy name to the men whom thou gavest me out of the world; thine they were, and thou gavest them to me, and they have kept thy word. . . . Holy Father, keep them in thy name, which thou hast given me, that they may be one, even as we are one. . . . I do not pray for these only, but also for those who believe in me through their word, that they may all be one; even as thou, Father, art in me, and I in thee, that they also may be in us, so that the world may believe that thou hast sent me (John 17:6, 11b, 20-21).

Is such oneness possible? I believe it is. At the expense of truth? No, but that the truth may be known, in all its fullness.

Herein are stories of souls, my own included, who sought the truth of God and of his Church, sometimes at great cost, even when their doing so seemed to go against what they had been taught, against what was familiar, against what they had come to trust, and against their very understanding of God. Each discovered that to be Catholic is not to have other than Christ, or more than Christ. It is, in the words of Augustine, to have the *whole* Christ, all that God gave us in giving us his Church. May their journeys strengthen the many who themselves have found the way home to the Church that has stood for two thousand years, and give courage and renewed determination to pilgrims yet on the way.

And to the millions of cradle Catholics who through years of struggle and change have remained faithful to their calling, faithful to the teachings of the Church, faithful to the worship of the God of Abraham—who gave himself *for* us on Calvary and continues to give himself *to* us as our daily food—we say thank you. Thank you, with all our hearts, for keeping the light on.

—Rosalind Moss
Editor

# 1

# The Break-In and Our Lady's Assistance

## *James J. Pitts*

I grew up in South Carolina. Mama had been raised Presbyterian. My father and his family before him had been Methodists for generations. Therefore my two sisters and I were doubly blessed.

Sundays we all went as a family to the Methodist church to worship God. But on special occasions, we walked across the street from our house to First Presbyterian Church for Bible studies, Boy Scout courts of honor, ecumenical gatherings, vacation Bible schools, and youth meetings. I've often wondered if there was a special destiny woven into God's plan for me in that he found a house for my family directly across the street from a church. My earliest childhood memory is looking out my bedroom window before dropping off to sleep each night and seeing perfectly framed in the window the illuminated facade of the church glowing seraph-like in the night, as if to echo Lady Julian's "All is well!"

On April 18, 1954, when I was almost one year old, my parents—believers in Jesus Christ—presented me for Christian baptism in the Methodist church. Baptized in water in the name of the Father, Son, and Holy Spirit, I entered that moment into the one, holy, catholic, and apostolic Church. It was encouraging to learn years later, while in the throes of significant life conversion, that the Catholic Church accepted my baptism of forty-six years ago as sacramental.

When I was a child there was only one large Catholic Church downtown, St. Anthony's. I wish I had told my mother before she died about the day I broke into St. Anthony's—but some secrets one just doesn't tell one's parents in childhood.

I was eight years old. It was a sweltering day in the middle of summer, and a friend and I were riding bicycles through a park. We conspired together to cross the "safe zone" set by our parents to see what it was like to ride downtown along the sidewalks. We crossed the perimeter that our parents had forbidden us to cross. And as we pedaled onto busy streets and experienced the rush of traffic, we could almost smell the adventure and taste forbidden fruit.

We rode until we were hot and tired. As destiny would have it, we stopped right in front of St. Anthony's Catholic Church, and were so thirsty we decided to break in to find water. Left to our own reasoning, we imagined this would technically be regarded as a break-in since we were both Methodists encroaching on Catholic soil. We agreed that Catholics would not forgive us our trespassing if they found us there.

So we boys hid our bikes in the shrubbery beside the church and, because of our inexperience in burglary, chose the front door in broad daylight as our target of entry. To our amazement, the door was unlocked. These foolish Catholics, leaving their doors unlocked that even children could break in, we thought to ourselves.

When the giant wooden door of St. Anthony's swung open, it made an impressively ancient sound, as if it had swung open for two thousand years. But at the sound of those authentic hinges, my friend got spooked. Down the front steps he ran.

"Where are you going?" I yelled.

"We don't *belong* here," he cried, not even looking back as he disappeared around the corner.

Once on his bike he rode like the wind, as I stood straddling the doorway, watching him ride to safety. "We don't belong here" I thought about that as I stood there between two worlds and was tempted to leave. But as I looked inside, I saw far beyond the narthex a stream of colors flooding into the church. Perhaps it was wonder itself that led me inside. "*Click*" went the latch: the great door which had opened with such fanfare now closed gently behind me. I was frightened and tried the door again to ensure I was not locked in. It wouldn't be smart for a Methodist to get locked inside a Catholic Church, would it?

The sensation of adventure pulsed through me again. I forgot the water I was after. And as I walked further into the church, the feeling changed to wonder and awe. There were dazzling colors everywhere—crimson, violet, green, gold, and silver—streaming in on shafts of light from the windows. I had never seen stained glass like this before or the effects of sun shining through it with such power. These Catholic windows had larger-than-life people and magnificent angelic creatures glazed into the glass. This communion of saints seemed to be coming boldly in through the windows as if this place were theirs to command.

Suddenly a childish question flew into my mind: "What if they can see me? Maybe they can sound an alarm!" I was afraid for a moment, surrounded by all these witnesses.

But then my eyes fell on the window depicting Jesus welcoming the children. His face was inviting, as if to say "All is well, my child." Words spilled from this window at the bottom: "Let the children come to me; do not hinder them." It was a surprise to see that the Catholics had used words from *our* Methodist Bible!

These beautiful windows came down low enough for me to reach some of the feet of the angels and saints. I looked up at their radiance from close range as they rose to a dizzying height. Time passed unnoticed as I walked among the windows to introduce myself.

Then I saw a woman—a statue of a beautiful woman in the corner of the church. She was tall, clothed in blue. The nearer I came to her, the more gentle and lovely she became. I looked at her for a long time. She was barefoot, as I was on that hot summer's day. I reached out to touch her foot, but then I saw the snake. She was standing on a *snake* of all things! I withdrew my hand. I wondered who she was and why the Catholics would allow a snake inside their church beneath the feet of so beautiful a lady.

What was that smell? There was a faint odor of something burning. I looked around to see a lighted candle glowing red in a glass chimney suspended by a chain from the ceiling high above. It was glowing near a strange gold-covered box. Attracted to the box, I stepped over the altar rail, but tripped and fell on my face. The clatter echoed through the church. I crouched on the floor for a minute and looked around at the saints and angels—good, they had not seemed to notice. I got to my feet and approached the golden box. I wanted to touch it and almost did, but something about it looked sort of Hebrew, like something I had learned about in Sunday school. Then I remembered all those holy objects of Israel guarded by God that, if touched by the wrong person, might strike him dead! So I didn't touch it—but I did wonder why Catholics did not know the rule that you can't leave a candle burning inside a church unless someone is constantly present in the room.

It was then I remembered how thirsty I was. Finding a side door leading down a long hallway, I looked and saw that the coast was clear. Still, I tiptoed as best I could down the hall until I found a cold water fountain. At last! As I leaned over to drink in the cold water, suddenly a firm hand came to rest upon my shoulder. Scared to death, I whirled around to find myself in the presence of a priest.

He smiled and said, "What have we here? Son, are you lost?"

Stammering, I told him, "No, I'm *Methodist.*" I was going to add, "and a Presbyterian, too," but he was laughing too hard to hear me. I felt some slight hope, because it was the kind of laugh that puts you at ease. So I told him I was thirsty and wanted some water, and that's the reason I had broken in.

He stopped smiling. "You *broke* in?" he asked, surprised.

"Yes," I replied matter-of-factly.

"Show me where," the priest ordered.

I led the priest to my point of entry, down the hall into the church past the dangerous candle and holy box and the beautiful lady and all the saints and heavenly hosts poised to come through the windows. I pointed to the front door.

"There," I said.

The priest looked at me, then at the door and replied, "But it was unlocked."

"I know, but I'm a Methodist and this is a Catholic church. It really *felt* like a break-in."

The priest threw back his head and laughed again, then walked me back into the church. I willingly went with him. He cast his eyes admiringly all around the church. Once again, I looked with wonder at the saints and a mighty sword-wielding angel, at the lovely woman standing on the horrible snake, at the crimson candle and the unusual box that had made me fall on my face.

The kindly priest stretched out his arms and gestured with his open hands to all that was rich within that sanctuary. As he did so he turned on axis as if to make sure he had embraced all things in his arms.

Holding the gesture, he said to me, "Son, everything that you see here, everything is yours. Don't ever forget this, that it's *all* yours. Now ... you'd best be getting home for supper."

I still remember the burning of the tears in my eyes and the unimaginable wonder in my heart as I turned and walked then ran out of the church, through the ancient doorway, down the steps and around the corner of the building. I found my bike, rode home, and never, ever told my family where I had been or what I had seen on that eventful day. The eight-year-old kept it in his heart for a long time. And to this day, it still feeds my soul as I ponder it.

Two years ago I was completing my second year as pastor of Westminster Presbyterian Church in Abilene, Texas. I was approaching the twentieth anniversary of my ordination as a minister. I loved the Lord Jesus, I loved being a pastor, and I loved the congregation I was serving.

In the summer of 1998, however, I sensed the need for renewal in my life, and I still had some annual education leave to spend. I remember how I wanted to come closer to the Lord. One morning in June, I read Psalm 42 in Morning Prayer:

> As a deer longs for flowing streams, so my soul longs for you, O God.
> My soul thirsts for God, for the living God.
> When shall I come and behold the face of God?

These words from the Psalms became the prayer God gave me to pray back to him: "I'm thirsty, Lord, like a deer running through creation, beholding your majesty. Now I've stopped be-side a brook. My sides are heaving so hard I can barely catch my breath. Lord, lead me to your River."

That very morning I remembered an Episcopal priest friend tel-ling me about a Catholic monastery with two houses of monks and nuns who lived on the same grounds and who offered spiritual retreats. I had noted the name and address of this monastery the year before; and when I went to retrieve it, I found it was Our Lady of Guadalupe Benedictine Abbey in Pecos, New Mexico.

I decided to phone them and was delighted that they could accommodate my wife, Sandra, and me on such short notice. The plan was that we would both go and stay the weekend. Then Sandra would fly back to her job, but I would stay for another week of spiritual direction. It was all settled. All that was left was for me to go home and tell Sandra what I had decided our dream vacation would be that summer.

"A *monastery*! Do you want to become a *monk*? Thanks for ask-ing me to tag along, but don't expect me to do any monkish things!" I understood this was her way of saying yes.

Midsummer found us at the monastery, and even Sandra en-joyed keeping the monastic hours of prayer and chanting the Divine Office with the Benedictines, though the incense made her sneeze. Hikes were invigorating in the cool of northern New Mexico, and after Evening Prayer came supper, then Adoration, followed by Compline. Then the Great Silence was kept until the Invitatory was intoned in early morning.

For the previous five years before taking the retreat at the monastery, I had been seeking a more sacramental life. I had al-ready come to believe in the Real Presence of Christ in the Eucharist; and, although I knew consecration of the bread and wine could not take place in the Presbyterian church, I was still hoping to lead my congregation to increase celebrations of com-munion together from once a month to every Lord's Day.

Because of my belief in the Real Presence, I received the Eucharist throughout my stay at the monastery. I realize now that canon law discourages non-Catholic believers from sharing in the

Eucharist except in dire circumstances, and even then at a priest's discretion. I did not know the Roman discipline then, so I received Christ's body and blood in faith with confidence in God's mercy and love. Furthermore, the nuns and monks were hospitable to me, and through them and the Eucharist, God opened an unexpected channel of grace.

The community scheduled Adoration from 6:30 until 7:30 every evening. I had no idea what that meant, and when I asked what exactly one does at Adoration, I was told that some pray on their knees or in their seats. Others, I was told, read and meditate. Some take pen and paper and journal in the Holy Spirit, all before the Blessed Sacrament.

That didn't exactly answer my question, so I decided to take my Bible and walk into the monastery chapel at 6:25. At 6:30, a bell rang and everyone knelt. I watched a priest walk toward the altar, pause, bow, kneel so low that his face touched the floor. Then he rose and went to a simple-looking wooden box. Somehow it reminded me of something I had seen before, but I couldn't remember where. He bowed again toward the box, opened it, removed a large Communion host, and inserted the host into a beautiful golden cross upon the altar. The host fit perfectly into a glass window at the center of the cross. The priest walked in front of the altar again and bowed as he had before. I wondered at this.

For a while, people were on their knees. Then some sat in their seats again to read or pray or meditate. I decided to read. But after a few minutes, I found myself drawn to the beauty of the cross and the host within it. A light shone down on it and it was radiant, as if the light were coming from it.

I went back to reading. Suddenly, a feeling of love and shame came upon me, and I had no idea why. I moved soundlessly out of my seat onto my knees and prayed to the Lord, but I could not avert my eyes from gazing on the host. I found myself asking forgiveness anew and asking, "How could I not know you were here with us?" Those were the words I prayed but I did not know why.

The next day, Sandra's long weekend over, she flew back home. I was to stay with the monks for another week. That morning a visiting Benedictine priest from England named Fr. Kevin was the celebrant at Mass. As he began the Mass, he begged our forbearance, explaining that this was the twentieth anniversary of his ordination to the priesthood and that because our Lady had been so kind to him all his priestly life, he wanted to dedicate this Eucharist to her. I was interested. First of all, that summer was also the twentieth anniversary of my ordination. Secondly, I wondered who the woman was to whom he had attributed such kindness. I looked around the room at the various nuns and female guests, trying to guess which one of them had rated from this priest such a fancy British title as "our Lady."

It was only five minutes into the homily that I realized who "our Lady" was, and I well expected to receive the full onslaught of Catholic Marian propaganda. I noted how sweetly Fr. Kevin spoke of Mary, almost as if he loved her. This irritated me and I decided to stay clear of this man for the rest of my retreat.

That morning the Abbot returned to the Abbey after a short trip away. He came and sat beside me at breakfast. He was a kindly man with a peaceable, calming effect on people. We sat eating cereal side by side. After a while he asked, "What do you suppose God is doing in heaven right now?"

Taken aback by his question, I wondered if this were normal Benedictine conversation at mealtime. I answered, "I suppose God's ruling in heaven." I looked at the Abbot, but he seemed busy again with his cereal.

After a long while, he looked up and said, "I believe God's doing a wonderful work of unity all around the world. Well, enjoy your stay." Then he excused himself to leave me to my thoughts.

After breakfast, I went for a walk outside. I wasn't watching where I was going when I rounded the corner of a building and I walked right into the unavoidable Fr. Kevin, who also wasn't watching where he was going. This unintentional collision of worlds ended with the priest knocked to the ground and me standing over him. I stretched out my hand to help him up. He jokingly said, "You're not going to hit me again, are you?"

Fr. Kevin got to his feet and, having me at a slight disadvantage, asked me a favor. He told me there was an exercise room with weight machines in the next building and asked me to teach him how to use them. I paused, wanting to refuse him, but went with him anyway. I found Fr. Kevin to be very teachable and humble.

Finally I could stand it no longer and confessed how I had not enjoyed his homily that morning and that I thought his devotion to Mary was unhealthy and much too sentimental. "You spoke as though you're in *love* with her," I said accusingly.

Fr. Kevin looked as though I had struck him in the heart. "Of course, I love her. She's my mother, the mother of us all. She's your mother, too, Jim."

I made it clear I didn't need his lecturing me about Mary, excused myself, and abruptly left the gym. "I will stay clear of this priest from now on," I told myself.

At noontime prayer, the Abbot was back to lead the praying of the Angelus. Of course Presbyterians don't pray the Angelus, and prior to that week I had never heard it prayed in my life. I was on my guard as the Abbot began the words: "The angel of the Lord appeared to Mary." The community responded: "And she conceived by the Holy Spirit." The Abbot led again: "Hail Mary, full of grace, the Lord is with thee. Blessed art thou among women, and blessed is the fruit of thy womb, Jesus. Holy Mary, Mother of God, pray for us sinners, now and at the hour of our death. Amen." There was something in the Abbot's voice that was so peaceable, so disarming, like a distant childhood memory of an ancient door opening and closing for two thousand years.

The Abbot continued: "Behold the handmaid of the Lord." And the people joined the Mother of God in surrender: "Be it done to me according to Thy Word." Another Hail Mary was followed by the Abbot beginning a slow bow as he intoned: "And the Word was made flesh." Then the community bowed as well: "And dwelt among us." A final Hail Mary anchored this prayer calling the whole world to remember the incarnate Christ. It also called me, personally, to open my heart to Mary, Jesus' Mother, whom I now realize that God has made to be the mirror of the Church.

On the second day of hearing the Angelus, I found myself moving my lips, then giving voice to the words. "They are from the Scriptures, after all." But my problem was not Scripture, it was Mary. What to do about Mary, I wondered. Why do these Catholics seem to have a whole dimension of spirituality that I know nothing about? I've loved God all my life. Is it possible that there's a Catholic world of truth that could easily subsume my own world, challenging it, completing it?

One day, I decided to go sit beside the Pecos River with my Bible and forget Mary. I decided to do my own spiritual direction for a while. I opened Matthew's Gospel to the first chapter. I was soon reading about the dilemma that Joseph faced when he was told that Mary, to whom he was engaged, was found to be with child from the Holy Spirit. Verse 19 says that Joseph was kind and just, and had decided against any public shame for Mary or himself. Rather, he would dismiss her quietly.

*Thank you, Lord!* Here was my answer, and straight from Joseph himself—I would not cause myself any public shame involving Mary and the changes in my life that devotion to her might bring. I'd just dismiss the whole thing. But before I could celebrate too much, I read the next verse:

> But just when he had resolved to do this, an angel of the Lord appeared to him in a dream and said, "Joseph, son of David, do not be afraid to take Mary into your house, for that which is conceived within her is from the Holy Spirit" (Matt 1:20).

I closed my Bible on the ground beside me. Then I closed my eyes. I saw a little boy walking through huge doors into an ancient church, passing beneath shafts of colored light into a hallowed place surrounded by the saints. I saw the boy approach a beautiful woman and touch her foot and look in wonder at the snake underneath: her Yes undid the No of Eve. I did not need to replay the whole memory. I found myself running toward the monastery to find Fr. Kevin to ask him to pray with me and show me how I might have access to Mary in my life.

When I found Fr. Kevin, he was working in the bookstore warehouse. I implored him to leave his work and come sit with me. He looked at me as if to say, "I can't believe this is happening," but he left everything to minister to me.

"Father," I began, "I've never *prayed* to Mary before. I'm not sure I'm allowed to *pray* to anyone but God. But I believe God is leading me somehow to make room in my life for her. I just don't know what to do."

Fr. Kevin sat still with me for a long while. He was praying. So was I. He broke the silence by saying, "You've lost your mother recently, haven't you?"

Startled, I simply replied, "Yes. She died four years ago."

"And you were a long way from her when she died."

Again, I was surprised he knew this. "That's right. We were in Hawaii. Mama was still in South Carolina when she died unexpectedly."

"That must have been very hard on your family."

I told him that it had been and that I missed her very much.

Fr. Kevin looked at me and asked, "Have you ever visited her grave alone and wished you could talk to her, tell her you love her?"

"Yes. I have been there and have had those thoughts."

"And did you begin to speak to her, when you were all alone at her graveside?"

That question made me feel self-conscious. "Yes," I answered, "I spoke out loud as if she had been there."

"As if? Don't you believe in the communion of the saints? That you are surrounded by a cloud of witnesses, of those who have passed from death into life, of angels and saints who are as united to us in their death as they were in their life, if not more so?"

"Yes." I could barely get it out. "But I never knew it was permitted to talk to them."

Fr. Kevin smiled, "You never thought it was permitted to talk with me either, did you?"

I suddenly remembered a kindly priest who once befriended me and told me that everything in the Church was mine: "*Don't ever forget this—it's all yours.*" I began to weep.

This English priest looked at me and said, "Jesus died, too. And yet God raised him from the dead, and to this day you pray to him. You *talk* to him. It's allowed, and he hears you. Just as your mother prayed for you while she was on earth, she can still pray for you in heaven. She lives, for she is connected to Jesus. Do you remember who taught you to pray?"

"She did."

"And aside from the fact that you knock priests to the ground every now and then, would you say that your mother did a fairly good job with your spiritual direction when you were a child?"

"She was wonderful to me."

The priest leaned close. "God entrusted your entire spiritual direction as a child to your mother and father—and they did well. What an awesome thing, that God chose such a simple girl as Mary, entrusting to her the entire spiritual direction of his Son. Would you say that Mary did a fairly good job of spiritual direction with Jesus?"

"Yes, she must have been amazing," I offered.

"Well, now, if Mary could do such great things with her Son, perhaps she could also do something with you."

"Yes," was all I could say. The priest took my hands in his, and for the first time in my life, I called upon Mary, the Mother of God, to lead me closer to her Son.

All this was an amazing uncovering of faith and the Catholic Church—to which God had mystically connected me in baptism and in a memorable childhood moment of grace. The power of Christ in the Eucharist and the intercession of Mary led me to open my heart to God in new ways.

This unfolded not without loss, for I loved the Presbyterian congregation that I eventually had to leave. I loved my work as pastor and all the riches of that ministry. But the invitation to conversion was for me to stand in that ancient doorway and surrender everything anew to Jesus Christ, Lord of the Church. It was for me an act of obedience to the Holy Spirit. First came my heart, and then my mind, and during Lent of 1999 on the weekend of the Feast of the Annunciation, both Sandra and I were received by confirmation into the Catholic Church by a good and kindly bishop in Alexandria, Louisiana.

# 2

# Return to Apostolic Traditions

## *Alex Jones*

On a hot August night in 1958, the Holy Spirit opened the doors to my heart. Since then I have been gripped by an unrelenting hunger to know and learn more about this wonderful God and his glorious Church. Who is he? What is he like? What does he want? What pleases or displeases him? Where do I fit into his grand plan? What has he done for others? These questions flooded my heart that summer evening and have dogged me ever since.

For forty years I have been on a pilgrimage to know as accurately as possible the purposes and plans of this marvelous God. Aside from my college studies and post-graduate work in education, I have read books, attended various church services, engaged in dialogue with Christians from differing backgrounds, argued with different sects, briefly attended a Bible college, and experimented with several variations of Protestantism. I have courted both Armenian and Calvinistic theology, embraced and discarded premillennial eschatology, practiced various forms of religious worship, preached holiness and sanctification, and generally enjoyed the spiritual experiences of my Pentecostal heritage. Yet underneath was the gnawing desire to dig deeper, ask questions, and find the will of God.

I found that wisdom quite by accident. It was during preparation for a Wednesday evening Bible study on the second chapter of First Timothy that I stumbled across this treasure buried in a field. Researching how to reenact a first-century worship service, I read the letters of the apostolic Fathers, and it was there that I unearthed a clearer understanding of Christ and his Church.

His Church was liturgical. It was hierarchical. I learned that as the Church grew, it kept a written record of lines of descent from the apostles themselves. Protestant claims of small "Bible study groups" scattered throughout the ancient world are pure fantasy. There is simply no historical record of them. The Christian Church was and has always been united, apostolic, and catholic. The rise of heresies forced the Church to cling tenaciously to what it had received from the apostles. All the churches from Gaul to India had a core belief and method of worship that all agreed could be traced directly to the apostles.

The center of Christian worship was not the operation of the gifts of the Spirit—which were in great abundance—nor was it the histrionics of great preachers. The center of Christian worship was and has always been the sacrifice of the body and blood of Christ, the Eucharist. To the early Church, the Eucharist was not a spiritual symbol of Christ, it was Christ himself being re-presented to the Father at every gathering.

Not only were the Church's hierarchical structure and Eucharist-centered worship different from what I expected, but so were its teachings. Men were not saved by accepting Christ as their personal Savior, but by immersion in the regenerational waters of baptism. Men were not saved by faith alone, but by the obedience of faith, a faith demonstrated in good works and holy living. Christians did not seek blessings; on the contrary, they willingly sacrificed their lives for their Lord.

But uncovering the historical beginnings and consequent development of the Christian faith was not enough to change my religious position. It was indeed exciting history, but knowing it only enriched my knowledge of the Church. It was the discovery of three incontrovertible truths that sealed my decision to give up all and enter the Catholic Church: (1) Christ's promise to His church of incorruptibility and perpetuity, (2) the unbroken transmission of Christian revelation in Apostolic Tradition, and (3) the consistent and universal witness of the Church Fathers, especially the apostolic Fathers.

## Christ's Promise of Perpetuity and Incorruptibility

As a Protestant I believed the Church was indeed the body of

Christ, but that it somehow occupied a position of lesser importance than that of the Scriptures. The Bible was *the* authority, period. To me the *real* Church was an invisible spiritual reality, known only to God, hidden in the multitude of differing church organizations, waiting to be revealed on that great Judgment Day. To me no *one* church could ever lay valid claim to be the church, because all those who claimed Christ were the church.

It never occurred to me that Christ left one visible, hierarchical church in which all of his fullness would subsist until the end of time. It also never occurred to me that this visible Church left an unmistakable trail from the upper room—where it was commissioned and empowered by Christ himself—to our own day. As I searched both history and Scripture, it became increasingly clear that Christ, before his ascension to the Father, left a living, breathing, legislating, growing, and developing body of men and women fortified with two irrevocable promises: *perpetuity* and *incorruptibility*. In short, Jesus left a living organism, not a written constitution.

It may not seem important on the surface, but it was extremely important to me to understand the beginnings of Christianity. It was important because it clarified the question of authority: who or what did Jesus leave as the authority for his new revelation? Did he leave a church or did he leave the Bible?

I think all will agree that Jesus left eleven men whom he called apostles to be the foundation and guiding force of his new revelation: "As the Father has sent me, even so I send you" (John 20:21); "He who hears you hears me, and he who rejects you rejects me, and he who rejects me rejects him who sent me" (Luke 10:16).

During the course of his earthly ministry Jesus singled out Simon, whom he renamed Peter (Aramaic: *kepha*, rock), and made him the head of the apostolic college (Matt. 16:16-19, John 21:15-17). Coupled with the promise to Peter of his headship was Christ's promise to his new community of indefectibility, or perpetuity. It would overcome all that Hades could throw at it and endure until the end of time (Matt. 16:18).

In short, Christ was saying that the community built upon Peter's administrative office (the "keys") would never be overthrown by external forces of persecution or corrupted by internal teachers of heresies. Satan would indeed try to extinguish this community with long and often severe persecutions (Matt. 10:21–22, 28) but would fail. In fact, during the five great persecutions beginning with Nero and ending with Diocletian, "the blood of the martyrs became the seeds of the faith."

Are we then to believe that Satan, failing to destroy the Church through years of persecution, would succeed in corrupting it? There were local churches that fell into heresy, but the one, universal Church remained true to the faith of the apostles. How could these scattered communities of beleaguered Christians remain true to their apostolic roots in the face of the second century's deluge of false teachers?

In a word, it was Christ's promise of the Holy Spirit's perpetual presence and guidance in the Church (John 14:16, 16:12-13). In their efforts to dilute the teachings of the Church, heretics would succeed only in "drawing away disciples" from the body; they would never be able to corrupt the dogma of the Church. All agree that Satan failed to destroy the Church with exterior persecution, but many seem to think he was successful in corrupting the Church with scores of false teachings and novel "inventions." But isn't defeat defeat? If Satan succeeded in corrupting the Church, the "gates of Hades" won! Instead of being the glorious bride of Christ without spot or wrinkle, it would become an unfaithful corrupt whore, detestable and vile in the eyes of God.

Unfortunately many Christians have adopted this view of the one, universal (catholic) Church. Certainly Martin Luther believed it and, in the years following his separation from Rome, he labeled the Church "the Great Whore of Babylon." But does such an assumption square with the promise of Christ to preserve the Church from error? What else could "He will guide you into all truth" mean?

Some say that this promise of the Spirit's "guidance into all truth" was for the apostles only. But how much sense does that make? Wouldn't the Church really need the guiding presence of the Holy Spirit *after* their death to ensure adherence to their teaching? Besides, what does "with you forever" mean? It was absolutely necessary that the presence of the Holy Spirit remain in the Church until the end of time, guiding it into all truth and around the perfidious errors of conceited men. And if he remained in the Church as a guiding force, how could it then teach error?

Scripture does not teach that the *Church* would become corrupt or apostatize from the truth. On the contrary, it teaches that *men* would either leave the Church or would seek, unsuccessfully, to corrupt it (Acts 20:29; 1 Tim. 4:1; Jude 3,4).

It is the *Church* that is the custodian of truth. The Bible as we know it was not the foundation of the apostolic Church. In fact, nothing of the New Testament was written until approximately fifteen years after Christ's ascension. I began to understand that God's method of giving revelation comes in stages.

First, he selects and prepares a people to become guardians of his revelation. Second, he unfolds this revelation to these guardians in its most basic form. Third, he makes these chosen custodians the interpreters of his revelation by equipping them with the necessary wisdom to understand and apply it.

Such was the case with Israel, the first people of God. God first called Abram, whom he would later call Abraham, and laid the foundation for a covenant people with great and gracious promises. Through successive generations God painstakingly built a nation from scratch and prepared them to become custodians of his revelation. He incubated them in Egypt for over four hundred years, then birthed them into freedom through the deliverance of Moses. For forty years he led and fed them through Moses, taught them by precept, disciplined them with trials, and chastised them with hardships (Deut. 8:1-6). Through Moses, God gave Israel laws of worship, a tabernacle, feast days, sacrificial laws, religious and civil legislation, an efficient priesthood, and governmental organization. They had not only the written Law but also the organizational apparatus to make it work. They did not have just the written Law; they also had accompanying oral instructions, which do not appear in the written Torah.

Moses committed these laws, statutes, and customs to the elders headed by Joshua, who succeeded him (Num. 11:24-25; Deut. 27:1; 31:3, 14; Judg. 2:6-7). These elders were eyewitnesses to the workings of God and accurately transmitted the Law they had received from Moses to the people (Judg. 2:6-7).

God's method is also evident in the unfolding of his divine plan through Jesus Christ. Unlike Moses, who was a faithful servant in God's house, Christ came as the son over God's house (Heb. 3:5,6). He was the promised prophet that Moses said would come to speak God's words to his people (Deut. 18:18; John 1:17; Heb. 1:1,2).

Jesus' first act was to find men, whom he named apostles, into whom he could pour his divine revelation (John 1:37-51, 17:14). They would become the new patriarchs and new elders of the new Israel, and the interpreters of the new law: the gospel mysteries (Matt. 13:11).

For three years Jesus labored with them in the truths of the kingdom. He not only demonstrated God's kingdom in power but also gave them firsthand experience in public ministry (Mark 6:7-13). To them he committed the organizational apparatus (the Church) and necessary instructions for administering it (Matt. 18:15-20, Acts 1:3). Just as God through Moses and the elders of Israel created an organizational system to clarify, interpret, and transmit the divine Law, so Jesus through the twelve apostles established an organizational system by which the new revelation was to be clarified, interpreted, and transmitted. Christ, the new Moses, brought the gospel, the new revelation, and committed it to the apostles, the new elders, who equipped the custodians, the Church, the *new* Israel (Eph. 2:19-20).

The bottom line is simply this: Jesus chose a body of men to lay the foundation for his new community, the Church. At Caesarea Philippi he gave the assurance of perpetuity, and in the Upper Room he gave the gift of incorruptibility. From these men arose the Church of Jesus Christ. It was unmistakably clear to me that if one could identify the church that stood in an unbroken line of succession from the Upper Room, one would have found the Apostolic Church. All other churches or ecclesial communities, however wonderful and spiritual their doctrines, would not and could not be apostolic. If a church cannot trace its teachings or ecclesial ordination to the direct line of the apostles, then that church—no matter how large, informed, or evangelical—cannot lay claim to being "apostolic."

Why is it important to belong to this "apostolic" church? Let me count the advantages: linkage to the apostles (apostolic succession); the assurance of truth; the presence of the Holy Spirit; the development and clarification of doctrine; unity in faith and practice with people from every nation, tongue, and ethnic group (one billion strong!); a Christ-ordained hierarchy of leadership united under one head who is the successor of Peter, the "administrator" of the kingdom; the truth about the Eucharist; Mary, the Mother of God; the intercession of the saints; and, finally, a coherent faith that encompasses Scripture, Apostolic Traditions, and historical authenticity. Simply put, this is the fullness of the Christian faith.

## The Transmission of Christian Revelation in Apostolic Traditions

With this clear understanding of the development of the Christian faith came a clearer understanding of the Bible and Protestantism's most treasured tradition, *sola scriptura*—the belief that all we need to know about the revelation of Christ and his Church is contained within the pages of the Bible. Hence, the Bible is the authority for all questions on faith and morals. We Protestants have shortened this teaching into, "If it's not in the Bible, I don't believe it."

On the surface that sounds admirable and correct: "If we cannot read it in the Bible, then discard it, it isn't true." But each of the 28,000 Protestant churches and denominations claims support from the one Bible! Each of them claims the "truthful and correct" interpretation of Scripture. From Lutheran, Anglican, Methodist, Baptist, and Pentecostal churches to Mormons and Jehovah's Witnesses, every last one of them interprets the Bible differently. We Protestants have grown so accustomed to this variety of interpretations that we call the Bible "unclear" in many passages so that we can allow for differing opinions and interpretations.

Take, for example, Jesus' statement to Nicodemus that he must be "born of water and the Spirit" (John 3:5). At least three interpretations have been offered by Christians: (1) amniotic birth fluid (the first birth) and the Holy Spirit's indwelling (the second birth); (2) the word of God and the Holy Spirit's baptism; and (3) the waters of baptism and the Holy Spirit's indwelling.

But Jesus' statement certainly had one meaning. Although it isn't spelled out in John's Gospel account, I'm sure Jesus explained what he meant to Nicodemus. But how does that help us? Which of the interpretations listed above is true? All three cannot be true, yet Christians build their faith on one or the other.

It doesn't matter how scholarly or erudite a Bible student may be. Even scholars who wear all the trappings of academia differ significantly on many important doctrinal matters. No amount of study and research brings consensus on what the Bible says.

Another problem with the Bible-only tradition is the belief that, with diligent study, the illumination of the Holy Spirit will unlock the truths of the Bible for all who listen to him (John 14:25, 16:13). Certainly the study of Scripture and the illumination of the Holy Spirit are essential to personal spiritual growth and to unlocking the spiritual content of the Bible. But try telling 28,000 bickering denominations that their 28,000 differing views on the Bible are an indication of their being either scripturally inaccurate or not Spirit-led.

Unfortunately, the apparently noble but unsubstantiated tradition of *sola scriptura* has limited its proponents to a narrow perspective of the Christian church. It not only limits the Christian's worldview of the development of the Church, its doctrines, its saints, and its history, it also does not tell the full story of the Christian church and its practices.

As depositories of the gospel message, the apostles had only their memories, aided by the Holy Spirit, and experiences to guide them (John 16:25-26). Moses had a written Law with accompanying ordinances and statutes, but the apostles, as far as we know, received nothing in writing from Jesus. What we call the Gospels would not be written for forty years or so after the ascension of Jesus and would not be canonized (recognized as official by the Church) for another 370 years. The Church, without any New Testament writing, was founded, organized, and set on its course. It was functioning quite well long before any epistles or gospels were written. In short, Christ did not leave a book but a living, functioning Church steeped in Christian teachings and framed with the solid leadership of the apostles (Acts 2:42-47).

Do not misunderstand me. The New Testament is the inspired word of God. It does contain God's will for us. We must live by its principles and commands. It accurately and faithfully relates the life of Jesus, his teachings, and the teachings of the apostles. But it must be received with the *total* revelation of the Church. The Bible is not the "pillar and bulwark of the truth" (1 Tim. 3:15)— the *Church* is! What the Bible gives is an accurate but incomplete picture of God's working through Christ in the Church (John 20:30, Col 4:17).

How did the early disciples conduct worship services? How did Christian worship evolve? What did Jesus teach his disciples on the road to Emmaus? Mark ends his gospel, "And they went forth and preached everywhere, while the Lord worked with them and confirmed the message by the signs that attended it" (Mark 16:20). But he does not tell us where they went or what they did. Acts reveals the beginning of the Church with tremendous power, but leaves us wondering about the outcome of Paul's trial in the twenty-eighth chapter. Nothing is said of the other eight apostles. Did they work miracles? Did they die for their faith? If so, how and where? What happened to Mary, the Lord's mother? How did the Church evolve after the death of the last apostle? What did Christ teach the apostles about the kingdom during his forty days before his ascension? How did the apostles baptize new converts?

Since the Holy Spirit was given to the Church to guide it in the truth, how was he evident in the centuries after Acts? In what directions did he lead the Church in the application of Christian revelation? What great men and women did he raise up to shepherd the Church? How did the councils of the Church deal with the practical applications of Christian revelation to the needs of the day? The Bible does not say. Consequently, viewing Christianity through the eyes of the New Testament is like trying to see New York City through a first-floor window of the Empire State Building.

Think about this. Limiting ourselves to what is contained in the Bible is similar to limiting ourselves to "mastering" the United States Constitution while ignoring the Fathers that created it and the history of the thirteen colonies that occasioned it. We would know the basic rules of American government but would be ignorant of the Bill of Rights, the great Supreme Court decisions that have interpreted the Constitution, the amendments to it, the slavery issue leading to the Civil War, and much more.

Consider this also: The Bible did not produce the Church; the Church produced the Bible. The Church is not built upon the Bible, but upon the apostles and prophets. Christ did not leave a written book to guide his Church; he left living men empowered by the Holy Spirit.

The New Testament, as we have received it, was not canonized until the year 393. What gave the Church its cohesion between the days of the apostles and the canonization of the New Testament? What determined orthodoxy of faith in the face of heresies and heretics? Why did the Church worship God the same way (except for a few minor variations) throughout the world? How could writer after writer call the Church "catholic" (universal) without the unifying element of the New Testament? What kept the Church afloat until the New Testament was canonized? In fact, what was the "rule" used to admit certain books and exclude others from the New Testament canon?

The answers to these questions are found in the traditions of the apostles handed down to the Church Fathers. This sounds strange to Protestant ears. We have been taught the Word has preeminence over everything. Yet we have ignored the very Church that has gathered, preserved, and produced the Word. Does the tradition of the apostles and Church Fathers have precedence over the Bible?

By no means! The Bible, along with the traditions of the apostles and Church Fathers, give us the *total* picture of God's work in and through the Church.

Jews understand well the place of tradition in their faith. The Torah was given by God to Israel at Sinai, but there was also an oral tradition, called the Talmud, that taught them how the Torah should be applied. For example, the Torah stipulated the times and types of sacrifices the priest should offer but did not always tell how the animal was to be slaughtered, dismembered, or presented on the altar. Judges were to administer justice, but the Torah did not tell how court was to be held. Engagements and marriages were to be held, but the Torah did not detail how or where the marriages were to be performed. The details and applications were handed down through oral, priestly traditions.

Apostolic tradition, however, differs significantly from Jewish traditions. Not only is oral tradition on an equal par with Scripture, it contains *all* that the apostles handed on to their successors, both written and oral—the total revelation of Jesus Christ entrusted to the Church. This sacred tradition (Greek *paradosis*, "that which is handed down") is transmitted from one generation to another as a sacred body of knowledge. It is the "faith that was once for all delivered to the saints" (Jude 3).

In Second Thessalonians, Paul admonished his listeners, "Stand firm and hold to the traditions [*paradosis*] which you were taught by us, either by word of mouth or by letter" (2:15). He wrote to the Corinthians, "I commend you because you remember me in everything and maintain the traditions [*paradosis*] even as I have delivered them to you" (1 Cor. 11:2). To some who refused his authority, Paul appealed to the universally practiced but unwritten traditions of the Church which had already begun to develop within his lifetime. In fact, he quotes teachings attributed to Jesus that cannot be found in the Gospels: "The Lord commanded that those who proclaim the gospel should get their living by the gospel. . . . If anyone is disposed to be contentious, we recognize no other practice, nor do the churches of God" (1 Cor. 9:14, 11:16).

Hence, the Christian faith began to grow well beyond the pages of what would become the New Testament. Customs, practices, traditions—all practiced and recognized by the apostles—guided the first-century Church through its formative years. Without knowledge and familiarity with *all* of the Church's teachings, the Protestant grasp of the Christian message may be good, but it is certainly not complete.

## The Consistent and Universal Witness of the Apostolic and Church Fathers

After the apostles passed off the stage of history, the work of the Church was continued through the bishops who succeeded them. Equipped with Apostolic Traditions, both written and oral, and the presence of the Holy Spirit, the Apostolic Fathers began the task of maintaining and clarifying the new revelation.

It was there, in the face of the Apostolic Fathers, that I saw the true essence of Christian spirituality. It was not today's Americanized faith of prosperity or materialistic blessing, nor was it the Pentecostal faith of endless exhilaration and emotional excitement. It was a deep, devotional faith of the heart that called forth self-sacrifice, penance, suffering, and righteous living.

Many ask, "Why should we study the Church Fathers? They were not inspired, so why read them or take them seriously? They often disagreed with one another, how can we rely on what they said?"

The Fathers would be the first to confess they were not inspired, as the apostles were. In fact, they often went out of their way to point out this fact. They never laid claim to inspiration. They confirmed and clarified the words of the apostles, but they never laid claim to inspiration. There are six reasons why I accepted the testimony of the Fathers, especially the Apostolic Fathers (104-125):

- They were the recipients and guardians of Apostolic Traditions;

- Many were witnesses to the teaching, preaching and practice of either the Apostles or their immediate successors;

- The entire Church regards them as authoritative and informative, though not inspired;

- They signed their witness in martyrdom;
- They sought to preserve faithfully what they had received from the apostles; and,
- They are windows through which we can see the Christian Church in its simplest, apostolic form.

The Church had a vibrant, rich spiritual life that was not fully captured by the New Testament. There were martyrs, great saints, great evangelism, and great examples of self-denial and sacrifice in the early Church that we do not read about in the Bible. The culturally diverse church at Antioch went on to become the driving force in Christianity. Great saints such as Polycarp, Irenaeus, Ignatius, Justin Martyr, Anthony, Basil, and the two Gregorys are unknown to most Protestant readers. The great thinkers of the Church—Origen, Tertullian, Cyprian, Augustine, Athanasius, Gregory of Nyssa, to name but a few—are totally ignored by the mass of Protestants.

Yet it was these men who withstood heresies and heretics, hammered out Christian thought, and formulated the very New Testament doctrines and theology we Protestants believe today. One must remember that the New Testament contains many letters (epistles) that were limited in their scope to indigenous problems in local churches. We therefore, unfortunately, get only a glimpse of Church life through those pages.

With all of this new enlightenment, I had to make the greatest decision of my life. Would I take what I had learned and resign from the pastorate of my church, or would I attempt to share an unpopular and alien message with those I loved, including the congregation I served? I chose the latter course, knowing full well that I would be rejected by many. Yet I am elated that I finally understand. It all makes sense. It all comes together. I do not reject the faith that nurtured me. I've simply expanded it to encompass the *fullness* of that faith! I do not condemn or belittle other ecclesial communities, because God has indeed used them to touch the lives of millions. We all are God's children, heirs of the kingdom. But I've found the Church of the Upper Room, and I will forever thank our Lord Jesus Christ for opening my eyes. I've come home.

[Alex Jones is accompanying fifty members of his former congregation through the Rite of Christian Initiation as they prepare
to enter into full communion in the Catholic Church at the Great
Easter Vigil in April 2001. —ed.]

# 3

# Through Deep Waters at Last

## *David K. DeWolf*

Dear Mom,

I confess I'm of two minds. How do I tell you more about why I took this step? On the one hand, I could explain to you why, in my own mind, remaining in the Presbyterian Church U.S.A. was unsatisfying to the point of being wrong. That runs the risk of exacerbating the feeling so poignantly expressed in your letter—that my decision was a rebuke or a rejection of the life that you and Dad have devoted to the Christian ministry. On the other hand, I could express it in the form of emphasizing those things that appealed to me about Catholicism in a personal sort of way, along the lines of saying that the grass on the other side of the fence looked greener, trivializing the sense of compulsion that I felt in taking this step.

Caught in this dilemma, I will admit failure at the outset. I think I owe it to you to explain those things that drew me irresistibly to the Catholic Church. In expressing them I may say some painful things, which I do not mean to be hurtful, but which (despite my best efforts to avoid it) may turn out to be so. On the other hand, I have to acknowledge that I am not without doubt about what I am doing. I have long asked myself whether this was just some kind of fad, a midlife crisis of a person whose taste runs to liturgy rather than to convertibles and the nubile receptionist at the office. Maybe I'll wake up at age fifty-five and ask myself, "Whatever possessed me to do that?" Even now, two days after the very joyous moments, I have a twinge of the unfamiliar, of a sense of finality, of doors having been shut, as well as a new one opening, the way it was on the day I married Priscilla. However happy that decision may be, it always carries with it the sense of loss as well as the beauty of all that it makes possible.

In your letter you drew upon our family tradition and my own growth through that tradition to the person that I am today. I took the liberty (I hope you will forgive me) of making a copy of the letter and sending it to John Jensen, the fellow in New Zealand with whom [my older brother] Charles and I have been in e-mail contact. John is an extraordinarily bright and deeply read man who became a Christian relatively late in life. He is now making a rather painful transition to the Catholic Church. Painful because he had been a founder and supportive member of the small Calvinist congregation to which he and his family belonged, and his decision to leave was pretty devastating to the community that his family had grown so close to.

John's reaction to reading the letter was to remind me how lucky I was to have been raised in a Christian home. I can't emphasize that enough in what I have to say. So much of what I now enjoy in my own spiritual life was made possible by the fruits that were planted when I was a boy. Some of it you explicitly planted in my heart and in my mind, through the many sermons and sermon illustrations that stuck with me over the years, through the Bible reading that we did. But it is characteristic of your own view of parenting that one has to raise one's children to be independent some day, and to your great credit I absorbed (through hymn-singing as much as anything) a kind of longing which was never fully satisfied.

I remember the tears that sprang to your eyes as you read a letter from Charles shortly after he had started his year abroad as an exchange student. He quoted the hymn *How Firm a Foundation*, and you got teary at the words "When through the deep waters I call thee to go." I always longed to be called to go through deep waters. I suppose it was in no small part my own prideful, ambitious nature that I didn't want to be a middling sort of Christian but wanted to reach for the brass ring, to be a disciple rather than just a follower. I wanted to be in the fast lane spiritually. I don't pretend that this was any great virtue on my part, any more than my desire to go to Stanford was any great virtue. I was given a great deal in terms of individual gifts and family and cultural tradition, and I always wanted to go the next step. Joining Volunteers in Asia, becoming a draft resister, joining the meditation group—I was always in search of something beyond the comfort zone. Obviously I made a lot of mistakes along the way, but I never gave up on the importance of continually striving to seek what is ultimately true, even if it is different from that which I have always believed to be true or which I find personally preferable.

Going to Gonzaga, a Catholic university, was of course not born of any conscious desire on my part to convert. I think I knew even before coming to Spokane for the first time in 1980 that there was much about Gonzaga that was post-Christian. I felt anomalous from the first, because I actually believed what many people had nominally agreed to but in fact had grown out of. I think there was an influence over time from getting to know more people who were Catholics, particularly priests, for whom I developed deep respect. There were others, of course, who were quite repellent. I referred to myself (even before coming here) as a "closet Catholic." I believed most Catholic doctrine because most of it is shared in the doctrine of both the Methodist and Presbyterian churches; only on a handful of issues (not well understood by most lay people, including myself) is there disagreement. Where Catholic doctrine differed, I often found myself in sympathy with the Catholic position rather than the Protestant.

The real reasons I never made a move toward conversion were: I felt Catholicism was just another denomination, with as many flaws as any other denomination; I felt I could never be a real Catholic because I was too ornery to submit in obedience to the teaching authority of the Church; and it was too messy to make the change—if it ain't broke, don't fix it.

One strong argument for remaining Protestant is to think that each religion is like the different members of the single body of Christ. We all have a different part to play; we're single blocks of color in the grand mosaic that makes up Christianity. No one of them alone is true; each is part of a greater truth. One can distinguish between the visible Church and the invisible Church, the communion of saints.

But if you take this to its logical conclusion, it means that we are responsible for our own salvation, that we shop for churches the way we shop for a grocery store, based upon whether it is conveniently located, has a good selection of merchandise, and has friendly staff. I don't take orders from my church; I select the church that fits my own preferences. Just as I am free to decide what is right for me, I have to recognize that others may see things differently and find a different liturgy or body of doctrine congenial to their disposition. Is there any absolute right or wrong? Are some churches that call themselves Christian in fact apostate? Well, they probably are, but that's not for me to judge.

Such attitudes epitomize the crisis of American Protestantism, and I found myself stuck in the middle of it. The PCUSA is split between those who want to make it more like the Presbyterian Church of America and those who are more like Unitarians with a Scottish accent. Please don't take offense at that crack. I have great respect for pastors like Jim Singleton and the fine fellow preaching at Lafayette Presbyterian Church. But the denomination is going through tough times.

Charles called me on it one day. He wrote, with apologies for the brusque tone, "Why are you still a Presbyterian?" I couldn't give him a good answer. The answers that came to mind were, "Because we have a good pastor at Whitworth Presbyterian Church." "Because I feel comfortable there." "Because I grew up in that tradition." But none of those answers is really satisfactory. I wanted to be able to say, "Because it is the true Church," but I couldn't. Is it enough to say, "Because it's a church, that because of my background and preferences, works for me right now"? I don't think so. It's the very thing I find so disheartening in our culture.

It's interesting that Calvinism itself wouldn't settle for such a definition. R. C. Sproul, my friend Bruce Gore's favorite Presbyterian scholar, is sympathetic to the Catholic position of saying that there is "only one gospel." Sproul believes that the Council of Trent forever marked the Catholic Church as a heretical church, deserving Paul's instructions in his letter to the Galatians that such should be anathema. Sproul thinks Catholics are wrong on the issue of justification by faith, but he's sympathetic to the insistence that you can't be partly right about such things; you're either right or you're wrong. Similar sentiments were held by the Reformed tradition.

Thus, I had three choices: I could be a loyal Presbyterian who thought this was the true Church; I could be a Lone Ranger Protestant, temporarily occupying a pew so long as I liked what was coming from the pulpit; or I could take seriously the Catholic claim that there was one true Church, and she was it.

Couple that with the sense of growing disquiet about that part of the Apostles' Creed that says, "we believe in . . . the holy catholic Church." That word meant for me that I had some obligation to act as though we really were one body in Christ, not a bunch of Lone Rangers in a kind of spiritual co-op where we traded with one another to mutual advantage but were always responsible to ourselves first and foremost. I heard some tapes that talked about the church as a family, and about the Reformation as a divorce within the family of Christ. It really hit home. In response to one of the comments in your letter, I felt a sense of urgency on this point. We live in a world in which people too frequently find that they cannot bear to live together any longer and they will be better off living apart. I judge no man (or woman) on this point, but I felt compelled to strive for unity rather than for separation.

I often have said that being a Protestant is like being a wife who has left her husband because he abused her (or she thinks he abused her). There is no question that leaders in the Catholic Church sinned in many ways, leading up to the Protestant Reformation. It may even be that, at the time Luther and others left, Protestants as a group were better Christians than those they left behind. But that is no different from a woman who leaves her husband because of some sin he has committed and who then refuses to reconcile with him because he continues to fall short of her expectations of what a good husband should do. There comes a point at which the unwillingness to submit oneself in obedience to a sinful husband is unbiblical.

Paul exhorted wives to obey their husbands, and he didn't qualify it by adding "at least whenever he's right." (Of course, he also exhorted husbands to love their wives, and he didn't qualify it by saying "so long as she deserves it.") Obedience always carries with it the certainty that we are being obedient to a sinner, whose sinfulness is likely to be expressed at least in part in the instructions that he gives us. Similarly, the Church to which I have been asked to be faithful is composed of sinners who occasionally demand from me something that is probably a bad idea. Bishops in the Church (including the Bishop of Rome) have made mistakes in the past and they will make many in the future. But I believe that our obedience, precisely when we are right and they are wrong, will be blessed by God.

It took me a long time to get over the feeling that Catholics were born, not made. I still feel a bit like a fish out of water, because it's such a complicated religion that it's easy to miss out on some instruction or piece of etiquette and to do or say the wrong thing. But over time I have recognized that it's a little like going to the school dance in junior high: other people seem so much more natural than we feel. It is only with greater maturity that we recognize that everybody feels that sense of being out of place. Those who pretend that they are at home are in fact becoming at home by that very act.

I have even become adjusted to the criticism and in-fighting that accompany any family. I remember the story of a certain family whose major indoor sport was telling stories at the expense of other members of the family—that is, so long as the one telling the story was also a member of the family. Woe unto the person from the outside who thought that it was okay to join in the fray. I feared something of the same thing as I joined this complex and sometimes chaotic family. But I have also felt very much at home. In fact, on the occasion of my entry into the Church I have been welcomed by many people in a heartfelt way. For me it is a plunge into a deeper spirituality and sense of community.

I think there is a fear that by becoming Catholic one surrenders one's autonomy, or checks one's intellect or individuality at the church door. I have to confess that there was an aspect of Protestant autonomy that I found distasteful, and many Protestants disclaim the kind of radical personal autonomy that has become the hallmark of our culture. In a New Yorker cartoon, the groom looks up at the minister and asks, "Forsaking all others?" Well, as a matter of fact, one's commitment to Catholicism is a similarly jealous one. One of the appeals of Catholicism was precisely the fact that it represents something more like marriage than, say, an agreement to co-sign a one-year lease. I wanted to graduate from the mind-set of the groom in the cartoon to the attitude of a man who couldn't wait to pledge to his bride that his love would be forever, for richer and for poorer, in sickness and in health. It is a fact that it might get uncomfortable down the road, that he might wake up in ten years and wonder if he'd made the right decision. But that very risk is what makes it so momentous and so blessed.

As a consequence I am reassured, when momentary doubt assails me, that just as God blesses marriage, he will honor this choice I have made. Thomas More on the scaffold was asked if he were sure that the executioner would be sending him to God. He replied, "He will not refuse one who is so blithe to go to him."

The last consideration was whether it was really necessary to do this. Rather than making such a drastic choice, couldn't I work from within, so to speak? How about reforming the good old PCUSA or else find another Protestant denomination, like the PCA or even some independent church, that would let me explore some of these feelings without crossing the Rubicon? Why offend your parents? I suppose part of the answer is that I was more and more drawn to this brotherhood and sisterhood in the Catholic Church. Quite frankly, I wanted to belong. It was like a lengthy engagement—one that leads either to marriage or to an end to the relationship.

One important belief that I came to hold is that the bread and wine during Communion actually became the body and blood of our Lord. I had always been moved by Communion, and the more I pondered it and read about it, the more convinced I became that this was not just a symbol of our Lord's body and blood, but actually *became* his body and blood. As I came to believe that, I came to want it for myself. Just as the bride and groom want full union with each other but must wait until they are joined by an act of will, so I had to await the consummation of my relationship with the body of Christ until I had joined the body of Christ through my own act of will.

This naturally raises the question of the standing of those who have not joined the one, holy, catholic, and apostolic Church. I am reminded again of Thomas More and his response to a question from the Archbishop about those who did sign the Oath of Loyalty to the Act of Succession. "I have no window into other men's consciences. I condemn no one. I only know that, as to myself, I will not sign."

God put it upon my heart that this was the next step in my journey toward him. He spoke through a variety of people who, in different ways, led me to the conviction that this was his will. I spent more than a year wrestling with the question. At many turns I met with obstacles, but in each case there was a grace that drew me onward.

I can only compare this experience to other conversion experiences in my life: I did not become a Christian in one night. I was converted on several occasions from a relatively shallow understanding or commitment to God to a deeper one. In Jim Singleton's sermon on Easter, he preached on John 20, and described Mary's turning around to Jesus when he called her name. I have always had a soft spot in my heart for conversion stories, and I always feel the desire to do it again. I felt him calling my name again this time, calling me—yes, through the deep waters. "But I will be with thee thy troubles to bless, and sanctify to thee thy deepest distress."

Love,
David

[David K. DeWolf said recently: "It seems like more than five years since this letter was written. Although I am still a few years short of fifty-five, I am more confident than ever that I will celebrate that anniversary with even greater gratitude for the grace which led to my entry into the Church. Though she remained neutral through my conversion experience, my wife Priscilla made her own journey the following year and joined the Church at Easter 1996. If anything, her enthusiasm and joy have exceeded my own. Three of our four children were received into the Church the following Christmas."—ed.]

# 4

# The Accidental Convert

## *Jeri Westerson*

"You did not choose me, but I chose you and appointed you that you should go and bear fruit and that your fruit should abide."

*John 15:16*

"Don't come back Catholic!" my husband called cheerfully to me as I drove off, headed to the town of Oceanside and the Prince of Peace Abbey.

I guffawed. Who *me*? Catholic?!

I was a Jew. But a Jew in name only. I called myself an atheist and felt like one. Raised within the tradition of American Judaism—a lot of religion but no faith—I was content. My life was going well. My marriage was great and we had a smart, loving son. I was attempting to embark on a new career as a novelist but had had little success so far in even obtaining an agent. But I didn't worry. I had confidence in myself that soon I would achieve.

My latest novel was about medieval monks, but I was having a hard time with it. The notion came to me to interview real monks to get a better handle on the main character, and so I got up the courage to locate a Benedictine monastery within a day's drive. I left a message on their answering machine and, not long thereafter, the Abbot returned my call. I wondered aloud if I would be welcome: Not only was my purpose the frivolous one of writing a novel, but I was a woman and a Jew. "Of course you're welcome," said Abbot Charles. "And to really get the feel of it, how would you like to stay a few days as our guest?" I generally don't accept invitations from strange men over the phone, but I figured, with a chuckle, that he was all right.

I was well prepared. I had a notebook, plenty of pens, a tape recorder, and a camera. I thought I might be able to expand my writing and perhaps write a magazine article too—something I had never done before. The nervousness returned and with it questions. Would they really welcome me? Would it be boring? Would I be uncomfortable? After checking in with the guest master, Fr. Sharbel, and leaving my things in my small room, I decided to take a walk on the grounds. As I approached the path to the prayer walk, I was slightly startled to come upon a life-size statue of Jesus. His arms were outstretched and he appeared to be standing guard over a little garden. As I gazed at the benign stone face, I began to consider: Just how comfortable would I be in this place, sleeping under a crucifix? I was not terribly comfortable with the worship of God within the context of my own religion, since I regarded atheism as a thinking person's approach to the physical world. How much harder would it be to be surrounded by crosses?

From my research into medieval life, I was well aware of Catholic liturgy and ritual, as well as of the Churchs checkered history, especially regarding the Jews. I had my own prejudices and misconceptions about the Church, as do most non-Catholics, yet when I arrived I felt strangely at home in this completely alien environment. I was glad of that, but didn't have reason to ponder it particularly at the time.

Giving an embarrassed nod to the statue, I walked forward and was met by a sight that abruptly and unaccountably moved me. This little garden was much more than a garden: in it were seven grave markers, seven simple wooden crosses standing amid the ice plant and verbena. There was no other indication that this garden was particularly special. It was understated, like the monks themselves. When I saw the seven graves, I realized fully that once they had come to the monastery, they would live out their lives and die there. I was profoundly moved by that thought.

Leaving the garden, I got to work right away. I recorded, took pictures, interviewed, walked the grounds, attended the Divine Office, contemplated, and wrote and wrote and wrote.

That night in my room while I readied myself for bed, I remembered the faces of the men as they talked. The mild and almost matter-of-fact devotion of these diverse men had struck me from the very first. Though I didn't understand or yet fully appreciate it, I admired their lives, their choices. I knew that their comfort was now in their utter devotion to God, but I was struck again at how completely they had surrendered their lives to an idea and a being that did not exist for me. Those seven crosses burned in my mind. I was content in *my* life. So what was it that I was missing here? And why did I feel so comfortable in this place and so alien with other Jews and Judaism? There was always something missing for me in the Old Testament. I couldn't relate to its message no matter how much I pondered it. This, in itself, was a frighteningly frank realization. It turned everything I had thought about myself on its ear.

Wait a minute, I told myself. What's going on here? Wasn't this supposed to be about monks? When did this become about *me*?

I lay in bed contemplating all the questions popping into my mind. Alone, in a barren room, one can do that. There are few distractions. I turned the light back on, sat up, and clutched my knees. When *did* this become about me?

Over my shoulder there was a metal crucifix on the wall. Years ago, the presence of such symbols had made me nervous, but I wasn't nervous now. Was it a mature appreciation? Familiarity? Something else? It might have been the place, so quiet and dignified. It was also the monks, so confident and certain. There is comfort in that, even to an outsider.

It was in the midst of these strained reflections that it happened. It is difficult to describe in words, though I have tried many times. But what happened was this: I felt a sudden, immense presence coming from outside and all around but also from deep within myself. It prodded and pushed from the inside outward. A voice that was not a voice said two simple words that were not actually words.

*Wake up.*

It was as if I were an empty vessel being filled very quickly. In that instant the atheistic Jew knew in every part of her frail humanity that this voice was not imagination, not a dream, but was the very real and unmistakable voice of the Holy Spirit of God.

It scared the hell out of me.

Atheism is difficult to describe to a theist. It's hard to relate to, because the atheist does not see what is missing in himself. I suppose it's a very selfish dogma—for me, it definitely was. It was only after this revelation that I could see the hollow emptiness with which I had lived my life; the reason goals had no real meaning once met; how I always had to keep striving for the next thing, the next rush, and sometimes—though this was not part of my vocabulary at the time—the next sin. I had lived my life alone in an empty room. But that night in the monastery the door opened, and though I could see no one, I knew with that prickly-neck sensation that there was now someone else there.

My mind whirled. It was incomprehensible. I simply couldn't be thinking what I was thinking! Was I having a religious experience? Worse, was I having a *Christian* religious experience? Could I be accepting not only God but also Jesus Christ? Not me! Yet these feelings. . . . How could I not accept?

Caution prevailed. It was late. I decided to try to sleep. Nothing was going to be settled in one impressionable day.

After a restless night, I arose at 4:45 A.M., the hour when the monks rise to get ready for Vigils, the first Office of the day. "Behold the cause of our joy," they chanted in the church. I gazed at the modern but slightly Byzantine painting of Jesus behind the altar. The sky was getting brighter through the windows behind the monk's choir, but I still saw the sparkle of Camp Pendleton's lights in the distance. The crows and the crickets were loud in the early morning light. I will hear what the Lord God has to say . . . .

I sat there as an objective observer, listening and taking notes. Yet at the breaking of the bread at Mass, my objective heart and mind were inexplicably opened wide, and in flooded a newness of emotion that I was unable at that time to comprehend. I sat there and wept without understanding, without truly realizing the full magnitude of what the Holy Spirit had done as he slowly drew me in.

When I left the monastery to return home, nothing was settled about my spiritual feelings, nor did I want or expect anything to be. Only time would allow reason to grow from confusion. But I knew that I had a lot more to think about now than just my novel. Spiritual awakening can be a slow process—or it can hit like lightning. And one tries to be cautious in a lightning storm.

On the drive home I wondered what my husband, a Christian in name only, would think about these feelings I was having but could not yet express in cogent thought. I decided to say nothing. I knew that the whole adventure of going to the monastery in the first place could foment an impressionable response. After all, I had gone to experience something, hadn't I? These feelings would probably dissipate in a month's time. All would be forgotten, like an agreeable dream, and only the sensation of something pleasant would remain.

But to my surprise the feelings were more intense even after that generous month I allowed myself. Like a persistent salesman, God had gotten his foot in the door, and he was pushing it open.

I finally confided to my husband. "Um—I've been thinking about converting."

Dead silence. It's interesting how many configurations the silent face can go through with all its many muscles. Cautiously he said, "You know that means accepting Jesus as the Messiah, right?"

"Yes. I do! At least I think I do." And then I said, "I'm—I'm also thinking about becoming Catholic."

"*Catholic!*" My husband's sentiments reflected my own. How could I accept being Roman Catholic? "Do whatever makes you happy, but don't do it for the wrong reasons," he cautioned me. He meant: don't get carried away by a love of history and a taste for liturgy.

But I had done my research. Even before entering the monastery I had concluded that the Catholic Church was the apostolic church, the direct line from the Apostles, and that all other churches stemmed from it. The Catholics were the only ones to have a Mass every day. That was important. It meant they took it seriously every moment. And now that this had happened to me as it had, I took it seriously, too.

But Catholic? I began to reread the liturgy I had downloaded from the Internet for my book. I started to read the Gospels. Also, I had to rework the entire novel. I didn't like its original story and decided to redo the outline. A lot more work.

Another month went by and I realized that the only way to solve this once and for all was to go to Mass and talk to a priest.

I looked up the nearest Catholic parish and wrote down its address. Then I hesitated. What was I doing? Was I going to turn my back on my ancestors, on all that I had known? Couldn't I just be inspired to be a better Jew now that I believed in God? But I couldn't shake the feeling that that ship had sailed. Jesus Christ was the defining difference now. What *did* I believe? I was being led, there was no question of that, but it was a convoluted road.

I drove by the parish church at every opportunity, even if my errand was taking me in the opposite direction. For a solid month I drove by that church, memorizing the strange 1960s brick architecture, the open block lattice bell tower, the beautiful stained glass window above the door.

Finally, in October, I got the nerve to go in. I sent my son off to school and then I made the short drive to the church. I parked on the street, not yet willing even to park my car in the church parking lot. I entered by the front door and stood in the vestibule, glancing at the booklets and announcements scattered across a table. I crept in and sat in the back. The missalette stood in a pocket in the pew in front of me, and I leafed through it just as the bell chimed and all rose.

I crossed myself—backwards. I could not kneel, not yet. Jews do not kneel in the synagogue. Kneeling was too foreign for me at the time. I didn't have to push all of this at once, I told myself.

The reading was from Paul about the conversion of the Jews. "All right already!" I said to a chuckling God. "I'm here, aren't I?"

And there I was again, tears of joy streaming down my face as they had at the monastery. Joy of the Mass, the words of welcome, the love and openness that I was just beginning to understand was Jesus.

I had to talk to the priest.

After the Mass I made my way to the parish office where I was greeted by the soft Irish lilt of Sr. Margaret, who said that Fr. Gerry would be back from the sacristy in a minute. What did I want to see him about?

I sat down, wringing my hands in my lap, my sentence coming out like one long word, "I'm-Jewish-but-I-think-I-want-to-be-Catholic."

She nodded, without changing her expression. I don't know what I expected. Was she going to leap from her seat, shake her head, and mutter, "No, no. I don't think so!" Was I going to be given a test? Or made to fill out mountains of forms?

Fr. Gerard McGuinness—Father Gerry as he likes to be called—took me into his office and listened as I told him the story of my journey. I needed books, I said. In books I was more certain. So he gave me two catechetical books, one a slim volume of basic questions and answers and the other a thicker tome by Bishop Donald Wuerl. I thanked him, said I'd read them, and left, grateful that the meeting had been relatively painless.

I went home with my new books and pored over them. Everyone knows that the Catholics are against this and against that, but I never before wondered: What are the Catholics for? With all my misconceptions, and my knowledge of medieval history, I still saw the Church as a medieval institution; I honestly didn't think with my liberal background that I could accept becoming Catholic. I'd start by looking into what Catholics are for, and then go church shopping. I'd find a church with philosophies I could accept. I leapt at Bishop Wuerl's *The Teaching of Christ* and challenged it. I'll bet the Catholics don't believe in this, I thought with some vehemence, and when I looked it up and saw that they did, I frowned. Okay. But I bet they don't believe *this*! Again, I was foiled. I read on. I was truly surprised—and incredibly pleased—to discover that the Church is indeed the thinking man's religion. This was not the Catholic Church I had ever heard of. Where had I been?

I couldn't accept everything right away, though. Like faith itself, God reveals slowly, illuminating through experience, waiting for the ripe opportunities for acceptance. Much of it was very hard. It took a complete turnaround in my thinking. They call that conversion.

I attended daily Mass. It was then that I started letting the rest of the family in on it. First my in-laws, who were like parents to me since my own parents were deceased. Then my siblings. No one was disapproving, but the question was always raised: Why Catholic?

The weight of superstition and misinformation bears down on the Catholic Church. I knew from my own study how wrong the naysayers were. But I had to go further. The fact of baptism reared its head and I—growing comfortable at the Mass and in this new skin of Christianity—came to the realization that I would have to be baptized. I do not know if the average Christian realizes the awesomeness of such a responsibility. It is the reality of the Jew that he is a Jew at birth and, except for circumcision, there is no further requirement but that of a bar mitzvah, both of which concern the male. You are born a Jew. This is recognized and vilified throughout the world and throughout the centuries. To believe suddenly in Christ is a hurdle in itself. That, in my eyes, made me a Christian irrevocably.

I saw listed in the church bulletin something about adult baptism classes. Classes? At first I thought, Why can't I just go down to the river and do it? But the more I thought about this physical act that Christians seemed to take for granted, the more frightened I became. Once I was baptized there would be no backing out. This was the Big Commitment. My fear and hesitation only made me realize how unready I still was for such a step. My history gathered around me. The voices of my ancestors groaned in my ears. Never had I been so Jewish as when I thought I was giving it up!

After several months of attending daily Mass, I got the nerve to phone up the parish's deacon, Ron Rehaume. I explained my situation to him and soon started the preparation program, called Rite of Christian Initiation for Adults (RCIA). He and his wife, Ellie, made the anxious situation comfortable, and I never dreaded a moment of it.

Some concepts came quite easily to me. Never once did I have trouble with the reality of the Trinity, nor with the Eucharist being the actual flesh of God. But devotion to the Blessed Mother and the saying of rosaries came harder. I didn't think I could honestly become Catholic if I couldn't accept all of its concepts. I'd only be fooling myself. It took time, research, and some audio cassettes by Tim Staples and Scott Hahn to get me into a proper frame of mind, to finally understand and accept the Virgin. The Blessed Mother and I, I finally realized, have a lot in common: We are both Jewish mothers and we both have remarkable sons!

I had not had much religious training as a child, but my mother had always celebrated the Jewish holidays at home, and I liked to follow them as part of my heritage, especially after my son was born. He loved Passover, Chanukah, and Sukkot (The Feast of Booths), and I took pains—as my mother had not—to explain to my child what it all meant. What was I going to do now? Was I to give up these traditions which had been so important to me as a child, to my son, to my parents, to my ancestors who sacrificed all to uphold their faith? But then Deacon Ron, the wonderful teacher of my RCIA classes, pointed out that the Scriptures have two testaments. It's not that we abandon the old; it's that the new is the *fulfillment* of the old. How wonderful! How many more layers of meaning can the holidays have for me now! Were not all the apostles Jews? Did they not wrestle with these very questions themselves? No wonder I could not embrace the Old Testament before. It wasn't finished!

Relieved, I got ready for my Passover Seder. Since the Seder is the origin of the Mass, the Last Supper, I thought it would be nice to invite Fr. Gerry, our retired resident priest Fr. O'Day, and Deacon Ron and Ellie to my Seder. Yes, it was unusual seeing the Roman collar above my gefilte fish, but it was comfortable, too. I got to break bread for my priest and hand it to him, very like those early Christians of the first century.

The time flew and I enjoyed the Easter season. I had never seen it before. I took the ashes on Ash Wednesday, wearing them proudly all day. Easter week was an eye-opening experience: Holy

Thursday, Good Friday, the beautiful Holy Saturday Vigil where the lucky few were baptized or confirmed. I was told that in some parishes one could not be baptized for one year, sometimes two or three. I groaned inwardly. I had come to long for Communion, to be fully in community with my new Catholic family. It was hard watching all of them go up for Communion, one by one, while I was not allowed to partake. But there was no choice now. No matter how long it took, I would wait.

Yet only a week later I was told that I was to be baptized at Pentecost! Fr. Gerry created a special vigil Mass for those of us to be baptized or confirmed. There was a small turnout, but I brought a dozen friends and family with me.

Wanting to symbolize how my new journey was joined to the old, I asked Fr. Gerry if it would be appropriate for me to be baptized in my father's Jewish prayer shawl. He saw no reason against it. So as I waited by myself in the church that evening, I was enveloped by my past while hoping in the future.

The baptism itself was startlingly gentle—no thunderclaps. But on receiving the chrism, and then the Eucharist, I was overwhelmed by emotion. (I believe heaven smells like chrism.) And I looked back with a new awareness at my life. Once it had been dull black and white, but now it was colored with varied hues I'd never before perceived. Now I could see how unuttered prayers had always been answered and I saw also how clever they were, continuously teaching me. I saw all the stages of my life, like a string of beads, and how God had led me to the only moment where I could accept him, a moment when I was at peace and not liable to attribute this movement within myself to some deep hurt or some merely psychological need. God had chosen the moment to open the door and would not let it be closed again.

I sit in the front pew now, no longer the stranger in the back, and I gladly receive Communion with my Catholic brethren. My son was baptized six months after me, and two years later my husband was baptized as well. In my first year as a Catholic, I became a lector and a Eucharistic minister to the sick and homebound. I joined the choir and became a CCD (religious education) teacher.

In my second year I became a cantor and youth choir director. And now I coordinate and teach in our RCIA program. It feels like a lot, sometimes too much. But Jesus said that much will be required of the person entrusted with much, and still more will be demanded of the person entrusted with more. I am so very grateful to have been brought home to the Catholic Church, but I recognize I have a lot of wasted time to make up for.

Oscar Lukefahr, in his book *"We Believe. . ." A Survey of the Catholic Faith*, says, "We can be fully human only when we believe in God." For the first time in my life, I feel fully human—and I don't mind it one bit. I try not to let a day to pass without special prayers for my monks who through their humble piety and generous nature started me, unknowingly, on an amazing journey into God's most approachable light.

# 5

# From *That Old Time Religion* to the Ancient Faith

## *Thomas Ricks*

When I was growing up in a fundamentalist Baptist family in rural North Carolina, Roman Catholics were about as scarce as hen's teeth. Unlike other Protestants I've known from the Northeast and Midwest, some of whom even went to Catholic schools, I didn't have Catholic neighbors or Catholic cousins. Catholicism was for me a religion which existed on television, in the encyclopedias I so loved to read, and occasionally in the dire warnings of Fundamentalist books about cults. In short, I didn't grow up in an anti-Catholic environment so much as in a profoundly non-Catholic one.

My father and grandfather were deacons in our small working-class congregation, and when I was about eight years old, my father entered the ministry and became a pastor, too. We belonged to the small Free Will Baptist denomination. (This designation had grown out of the 18th-century controversies among Baptists over the free will of man. Those who followed the Calvinist tradition—that each person is destined from all eternity for either salvation or damnation and has no active role in that destiny—became Particular Baptists, Primitive Baptists, Missionary Baptists, and eventually, the Southern Baptist Convention. Those who asserted that man was completely free to accept or reject God's offer of salvation became General Baptists and Free Will Baptists.)

My family's life revolved around church activities, and most of my childhood memories involve religion in one way or another. Except for sickness, there was absolutely no excuse for missing church services—not only on Sunday morning, but on Sunday and Wednesday evenings as well. Twice a year we had a revival: a weeklong series of nightly services that usually featured the preaching of a fiery evangelist. My father was quite a pulpit-pounder, and, once he had entered the ministry, he received lots of invitations to preach revivals for other congregations. So my brother and I went to more than our share of revival services. These would usually culminate on Sunday with a wonderful church dinner and sometimes a gospel music concert that lasted all afternoon. I chuckle when I think of Fundamentalist criticisms of Catholics drinking—because I remember the gluttony we all committed at those church dinners!

I thank God whenever I consider the upbringing that I had in those Fundamentalist churches. Sometimes people from backgrounds like mine remember their childhood religion as severe or overly legalistic, but my experience was different. I can't remember a time when I didn't know that God loved me so much that he became incarnate, died to redeem me, and arose as victor over sin and death. Certainly the God I was introduced to as a child was, in the Old Testament phrase, "a jealous God," who demanded holiness of life and whose commands were exacting. But he was also presented to me as a God of infinite mercy who cared about the details of our lives. It was as natural in our church to pray for a new job for someone who had been laid off as it was to pray for more spiritual things. We were even privileged to witness a few genuine medical miracles.

Needless to say, this fervent spiritual environment made a deep impression on me. I made a profession of faith in Christ and asked to be baptized a few months after my eighth birthday. Baptists baptize by complete immersion only, and since our congregation's baptistry had a leak and needed repair, our church held baptisms outdoors. These were wonderful affairs. We would gather by old Doctor Putney's pond on Sunday afternoon and sing hymns without accompaniment. Then those who had recently gotten saved would be walked out into the little lake and immersed. When it was my turn, I came up out of the water spluttering, but certain that I was saved and headed for heaven. Not that we believed that baptism conferred grace, mind you: for the Baptist, baptism with water is merely an outward profession of something interior which has already taken place.

When I was about fifteen, I began to feel a call to teach and preach the gospel myself. I was given the opportunity to conduct youth evangelization, usually in the form of "Youth Revivals," and soon I was filling in on occasional Sunday mornings for pastors who were away, including, of course, my own father. Sometimes my opportunities to preach came up unexpectedly. I remember one Wednesday afternoon when I came home from school about four o'clock to find that my father, never one to miss a day of work, had been in bed sick all day. "You're going to have to preach tonight," he said weakly. And I did.

It will no doubt seem odd to Catholics or mainline Protestants to imagine a teenage boy preaching, but this has to be placed in the context of the Fundamentalist preaching tradition. For Catholics, preaching is a liturgical act in which a trained homilist presents an explanation of the Mass readings, especially the Gospel, and their application to Christian life. For Fundamentalists of the type I grew up among, preaching is more in the tradition of prophecy: God calls someone through whom he wishes to proclaim his will, and that person is empowered to do so by the Holy Spirit. This is why we often referred to the sermon as "the message" or "a word from the Lord."

As a matter of fact, many of the Fundamentalists I grew up among would take a preacher's youth, inexperience, or lack of education as signs of a "calling." If sound and useful preaching came from a completely unexpected source, wasn't it evidence that the Holy Spirit was speaking through that person? This led to an unfortunate lack of regard for theological training and spiritual formation, but it also led to some interesting opportunities for God's grace to work in spite of human weakness. (After my conversion to Catholicism, I was delighted to discover that my sermon on the Lord's Prayer, written when I was about nineteen, contained an exegesis almost identical to that in St. Louis de Montfort's *The Secret of the Rosary*. God sometimes puts good wine in lowly vessels.)

In college I served as interim pastor of two small congregations and continued to "supply" for absent ministers. During this time I also met the woman who would become my wife. Melissa's spiritual background was somewhat different from my own. She had been raised in the United Methodist church. Finding modern mainline Protestantism intellectually unsatisfying, she had drifted into agnosticism for several years. By the time I met her, she had come back to faith in Christ in an evangelical Baptist setting. The congregation in which we met was part of the Southern Baptist Convention, and I eventually changed my affiliation to that much larger denomination.

Melissa was completely supportive of my efforts in ministry, and during our engagement we became part of a group that founded a new congregation. The new church was part of the "cell church" movement, in which every member would belong not only to the congregation but also to a smaller group that would meet regularly for prayer and mutual encouragement. The idea was that each "cell" would nurture the spiritual life of each of its members, while at the same time serving as a focal point for evangelization. We were determined to return to the primitive Christianity of the first-century believers. I had plenty of opportunities to preach during our Sunday celebrations and I also undertook the leadership of one of the cells.

Though Roman Catholicism was the furthest thing from my mind during most of my childhood and after I began preaching the gospel, over the years a number of nagging doubts about our Baptist faith had entered my mind. The source of many of my doubts was the Bible itself—there were simply too many passages of Scripture that contrasted with our doctrine and practice. Christ's words in John 6 and those of St. Paul in 1 Corinthians 11:27-30 made me wonder if just maybe there was supposed to be more to Holy Communion than our symbolic bit of unleavened bread and our plastic thimbleful of grape juice. The organization of the early Church described in the New Testament, with its bishops and presbyters, did not seem to have much in common with our system of elected deacons, hired ministers, and denominational committees. And what on earth could Paul have meant about making up in our own bodies what was lacking in the sufferings of Christ? Furthermore, why did the Catholic Church have that annoying way of popping up so often during my studies of history? Christ had made a promise that the gates of Hades would not prevail against his Church, and clearly the Baptist faith was the biblical one. So where had the Baptists been prior to the sixteenth century?

It was quite easy to push such questions to the sides of my mind, especially when I was busy with the exciting work of preaching and of helping to build a "new work" for the Lord. So Melissa and I married with the expectation that I would complete my education and then I would go on to join the full-time staff of our new congregation or else follow God's call wherever it might lead. Melissa, the former agnostic and feminist, was content to settle into the role of the Baptist preacher's wife.

One month after we returned from our honeymoon, I went away to a weekend conference which, although religious in nature, was not theological. It was sponsored by an organization whose mission is to educate clergy of all faiths in the moral and philosophical underpinnings of the free market system. Although founded by a Catholic priest, the organization was completely ecumenical. This conference was to focus exclusively on political and economic questions considered in the light of religious faith, not on doctrine. Little did I know how profoundly my attendance at this conference would change my life.

God chose that conference as the time and place when all my suppressed doubts and questions would be brought to the forefront of my mind, so that I felt acutely the need to answer the questions I had been ignoring. I was practicing, and even teaching others to practice, a form of Christianity which I could not with certainty identify as having existed before the sixteenth century. It would be intellectually dishonest to let the Catholic Church's claim of apostolicity go unanswered. At that conference, for the first time in my life, I met devout and informed Catholics who lived their faith deeply and knew exactly why they were Catholics. Their knowledge of the Scriptures and their patient, charitable, firm replies to my challenges impressed me greatly.

On Sunday I attended the Mass celebrated for Catholics at the conference. It happened to be the Feast of Corpus Christi. Fr. John Michael Beers of Mount Saint Mary's Seminary celebrated the Mass, and his brief homily—which lasted only a few minutes—quoted Augustine on the Eucharist.

During that homily, and throughout the rest of the Mass, I had a strange interior experience. I sensed a unity among those present, and a Reality on that altar, in which I did not share. It was as if I were being pulled backward and away from something beautiful and powerful but altogether foreign to me. A friend I had made during the conference and with whom I had spent a good deal of time debating and discussing the faith reminded me, years later, that after the Mass I had said to him, "I've just witnessed either the fullness of the Christian faith—or the most vile pagan ritual that ever took place."

On the way home from the conference, as I contemplated describing my experiences to my new bride, I felt fear and trepidation. Would she be angry? Upset? Would she think I was ridiculous? Would she feel that she had been duped by entering a marriage in which I had suddenly changed the rules after a month?

Melissa picked me up at the airport, and I worked up enough nerve to bring up the subject right away, knowing that there was no way to soften the shock. As we drove down the highway, I swallowed hard and began, "Some very unusual things happened to me this weekend. Now I want you to hear me out about this, and I don't want you to get upset or leave me by the side of the road or anything, but . . . well, I think . . . I think that, for whatever reason, the Holy Spirit is leading us to consider Roman Catholicism." I held my breath, having no idea whether her response would involve tears, laughter, or silent shock.

"Well," she said, "we believed when we married that you are to be the spiritual head of our household. So if the Lord is leading you in this way, as far as I'm concerned, he's leading me, too. I don't need some kind of special, personal revelation."

The tables had been turned: She was the one who was shocking me, rather than the other way around. To this day I am still awed and humbled at the interior calm, the faith in God, and the confidence in me her response revealed. At the time, we had no concept of Marian devotion, but I have never witnessed a better reflection of the Blessed Mother's attitude at the Annunciation than my wife exhibited on that day.

As we began to talk through the enormous ramifications of conversion, we agreed on two policies. First, we would do nothing, make no decision one way or the other, for a period of five years. (The joke was on us: We were received into the Catholic Church eighteen months after making that decision.) Second, neither of us would convert without the other. We were going to have unity in our home, at all costs.

Thus began the most emotionally and intellectually intense period of our lives so far. We took a three-part approach to our consideration of whether to convert to Catholicism. First, we tried to read the Scriptures afresh, with our hearts and minds as open as possible. With my background, it was difficult to read the Bible without bringing along a huge amount of interpretive baggage. But as I began to read anew, I was amazed at all the things I was now seeing in the New Testament, things to which I'd always turned a blind eye because they did not fit the Fundamentalist/Evangelical system to which I had been committed and in which I was comfortable. Suddenly, the Petrine primacy was all over the place. The prominence of the sacraments, particularly the Eucharist, leapt off the pages. There were passages I'd glossed over a hundred times which I now realized were extremely difficult to reconcile with the twin Protestant pillars of *sola scriptura* and *sola fide*.

Second, we studied Catholicism. We knew that there were holes a mile wide in our knowledge of Catholic belief and practice. We joined an informal inquiry group at the local Catholic parish. Whenever we traveled, we would attend a Mass instead of going to a Baptist service, always sitting in the front pew if possible and carefully observing every detail. A few months after we began our search, we met Fr. Conrad Kimbrough, a parish priest in the diocese of Charlotte, through what I believe to be providential circumstances. This holy and wise priest, a convert himself, would prove to be instrumental in our conversion.

Third, we read the writings of the early Church Fathers. There was really only one question for us: What was the religion of the apostles and the other early Christians? That is what we wanted for ourselves, whether it meant remaining Baptists, becoming Catholics, or entering upon some third way we hadn't even considered. As I began to read works like the *Didache, The Apostolic Tradition* by St. Hippolytus, the Epistle of St. Clement of Rome to the Corinthians, and the works of St. Irenaeus, I grew more and more amazed. So many doctrines and practices that I had assumed were medieval accretions—from the veneration of saints to intercession for the dead to the baptism of infants—were clearly traceable to antiquity.

More and more I began to see that our "cell" church's practice of the faith, while well intentioned, was very different from the practice of the early Christians we had been trying to emulate. Then I came across the seven epistles of St. Ignatius of Antioch, and my last defenses were shattered. Ignatius, who was martyred in about 107, wrote the epistles as he was being taken from his diocese to Rome to be thrown to the lions. His testimony was a powerful witness to me because he lived, taught, and was elevated to the office of bishop at such an early time in the history of the Church, and he had probably known the apostle Peter personally. Yet even then, at the very beginning of the second century, he writes emphatically and profoundly of both the Real Presence in the Eucharist and of the essential importance of Apostolic Succession. Once I had read those seven epistles, there was really no turning back. I wanted to be in the same Church as Ignatius.

On January 1, 1994, on the Feast of Mary, Mother of God, my wife and I and our six-month-old son entered the Catholic Church. At the noon Mass, Melissa and I were conditionally baptized, and we received our first Holy Communion. During the evening Mass, our son was baptized and we were confirmed. I took the name Ignatius, in tribute to the role that the great bishop and saint had played in my conversion. Melissa took the name Mary Monica, honoring the two great mothers of the Church, in acceptance and celebration of her vocation as a Catholic wife and mother.

We had kept our consideration of Catholicism secret until just a couple of months before we were received into the Church, not wanting to rock the boat among our family and friends until we knew for certain whether we were going to take such a momentous step. One of the more humorous and poignant aspects of our conversion was the various reactions we received. When we broke the news to our Baptist pastor—who remains a close friend to this day—he looked at me and said, "You're as stubborn as a mule, so I'm not going to even try to change your mind." I just smiled, but I was thinking, "I've just admitted that I've been wrong for most of my life about the very nature of God's Church; I've given up my preaching ministry; I've risked the alienation of those closest to me . . . and *I'm* the stubborn one here!"

A close relative of Melissa's, an honorable, elderly gentleman for whom I have deep respect, said when we told him of our conversion, "You know, I've read the Bible through many times, and according to it, Catholics are the only ones with the true religion." As we sat in shocked silence, he added off-handedly, "But I've been a Methodist my whole life and I guess I always will be." When Melissa visited a former colleague of hers, a Mormon, and told her of our intention to convert, the woman replied, "I didn't know you could *become* a Catholic—I thought you had to be *born* one!"

Shortly after we entered the Church, a local Catholic woman whom I knew slightly said something that puzzled me deeply. She was approaching me in order to chastise me for praying publicly for the conversion of Protestants (the zeal of the new convert!), but she began by welcoming me into the Church. Having heard a little about our background and our conversion from mutual friends, she said, "I understand that your conversion involved a certain amount of tearing, and I hope there has been some conso-

lation for that." I couldn't imagine what she was talking about—
how could receiving the body and blood of Christ fail to be overwhelming consolation for any puny sacrifices I had made? She
didn't understand that I felt like a man who has been living on
bread and water his whole life and who discovers that the most
sumptuous banquet imaginable is taking place right next door—
and that he is invited. For me, the bread and water had been fine,
so long as I knew of nothing better, and it had certainly kept me
alive, but now, in the sacraments and in the liturgy, I was tasting
the finest meats, the freshest salads, the choicest wines. I was like a
man who all his life has been told that he must build a house but
has never been given a hammer and a saw. Now, in the Divine
Office, the rosary, the stations of the cross, and Eucharistic adoration, I had discovered a whole treasure-trove of tools. Consolation,
indeed!

Since we've entered the Church, God has blessed us with three
more children, each baptized in turn by Fr. Kimbrough, who is
truly our father in the faith. We have lived in California, Texas, and
now Virginia, and have met many fine and faithful Catholics
everywhere we have been. We have known many other converts,
and in every conversion story that I hear there is something
unique. Each story is completely different from our own journey,
and yet each is utterly familiar. I still thank God for the precious
truths that I learned in my Fundamentalist upbringing. Although I
have deep admiration for many of the cradle Catholics we know, I
often wonder whether my own background was a mercy of God,
given to me to protect me from the confusion and disorder the
Church has struggled with over the last few decades and which,
perhaps, I would not have been able to withstand.

And, of course, the story is not finished. Entering the Catholic
Church was, in a sense, the beginning of our pilgrimage rather
than its end. As my wife and I, amid the rigors of living as
Catholics in our times, take up the challenge of raising genuinely
Catholic children and face the daunting task of simply growing
in grace, we are comforted by the examination of the Church's
history that we made during our time of conversion. For two

thousand years, our Lord has come to his people in the Blessed Sacrament, making them—whether rich or poor, scholarly or illiterate, powerful or obscure—into saints. Sometimes I catch myself whistling the old hymns I loved as a child, and then I smile and realize that they were often right: God's grace is indeed amazing, and there really is power in the blood.

# 6

# Surviving Evangelical Burnout

## *Howard Charest*

In the midst of a wild theological discussion shortly after I became Catholic, some Evangelical acquaintances asked me what I had gained by converting to Catholicism. My response was as true then as it is now, twelve years later. I had embraced Evangelicalism for about five years, but its theological and spiritual inadequacies had contributed to my nearly losing faith in Christ. Catholicism restored and deepened both my faith in and my love for Christ, and, in so doing, began to fulfill my deepest spiritual and intellectual longings.

Raised first as a Lutheran and then as a Presbyterian, by the time I finished high school, I had become an atheist of the scientific humanist sort. Scientific objections to Christianity, such as evolutionary theory, had been my primary stumbling block. But within a year of graduating from high school, I faced a personal crisis concerning the meaning of life. I made a commitment at that point to embrace truth wherever it might be found and subsequently came upon the book *How Should We Then Live?* by the Evangelical thinker Francis Schaeffer.

His reasoned critique of humanism led me to grasp the full implications and internal contradictions of the atheism I espoused, especially in regard to the ultimate meaninglessness and absurdity of atheistic existence. His spirited defense of Christianity opened my heart to the gospel, and, recognizing myself as a sinner and morally guilty before God, I believed that through Christ's sacrifice my sins had been forgiven. I identified my conversion experience as the "born-again" experience I had heard so much about during high school, and my attitudes toward life truly began to change.

Schaeffer's interpretation of Christianity left a mark on me. On the positive side, I gained an interest in defending Christianity intellectually (especially through philosophy) and a fascination with the history of theology, philosophy, and culture. On the negative side, Schaeffer left me with the conviction that true Christianity equals Reformation Christianity, represented in the modern world by Evangelicalism. For the next five years I would assume, virtually without question, that Christianity stands or falls with Evangelicalism. However fascinating the Catholic intellectual and spiritual tradition might appear to be—and during the next few years I occasionally would feel a pull in that direction—intellectually I was convinced that Catholicism was an apostate religion, especially in its understanding of the way of salvation.

Yet it was the expectations concerning Christianity raised by Schaeffer that ultimately would make my departure from Evangelicalism necessary. These expectations are best expressed by something Schaeffer wrote in *The Church at the End of the Twentieth Century*. He explained that Christianity was the true and highest mysticism, for it is a personal relationship with God, which is grounded in rationality. In other words, Christianity is a rational answer to the question of the meaning of life, one which fulfills man's deepest spiritual longings and resolves his deepest spiritual problems. Two developments would lead me to conclude that Evangelicalism could not fulfill these expectations and that, if Evangelicalism really did equal Christianity, I should have to abandon Christianity.

First, the spiritual activism of Evangelicalism would contribute to my having a spiritual burnout: a mental exhaustion in regard to spiritual practices and activities. Second, my confidence in the Evangelical way of life was seriously undermined and my burnout consequently intensified as I came to believe that Evangelical thought, based ostensibly on the Bible as its sole authority, was incapable of meeting the many intellectual challenges facing it. I would come to the conclusion that Schaeffer's defense of Reformation Christianity had serious limitations even though his critique of humanism contained important insights.

Ultimately, and much to my surprise, I would find that it was the Catholic intellectual tradition that fit Schaeffer's glowing descriptions of Christianity's intellectual viability, and it was Catholic spirituality that most adequately fulfilled the Christian mysticism Schaeffer had hinted at.

After my initial conversion experience, my first Evangelical involvement was as a member of a Lutheran church. I remained a Lutheran for two years and then, through the influence of Campus Crusade for Christ, I left to become a Baptist. Looking back, I realize that part of my discontent with Lutheranism came from the fact that while Lutheranism acknowledges the importance of doing good works, it seems more interested in consoling sinners than in showing them how to overcome sin. One of the benefits of being a Catholic, I have now found, is a spiritual discipline centered around mortification and penance—a discipline that is powerful in overcoming sin.

In the same year of my conversion, shortly after I joined the Lutheran church, I became involved in Campus Crusade. At first Campus Crusade benefited me greatly, both spiritually and socially. The Crusade's emphasis on a Spirit-filled life helped me grow in personal character, and I was encouraged to spend time reading the Bible daily. This I loved to do, and I became an avid student of Scripture, eventually beginning to study Greek in order to draw closer to the meaning of the New Testament. In addition to these spiritual benefits, the Crusade's emphasis on evangelism and discipleship helped me learn to communicate my beliefs with boldness, and through the love and acceptance I found in this group, I progressed considerably in social maturity.

I immersed myself in the Crusade way of life, evangelizing frequently and conducting small discipleship groups. One semester I led the Crusade group at a local community college. But the overall spirituality and practice of the Crusade—which, I would discover, is fairly typical of large segments of Evangelicalism—worked to generate within me the spiritual burnout that would almost destroy my Christian life.

The major cause was Campus Crusad's emphasis on activity. I

found that the genuineness of one's spirituality was measured by one's involvement in evangelism and discipleship. I grew to assume that if I did not have a personal ministry, I was not living the true Christian life. This intense focus and activity-centered Christianity would have a corrupting influence on me—an experience that is, I believe, is shared by many Evangelicals. For example, the need to find opportunities to share our faith and win disciples would lead us to develop friendships with people, Christians and non-Christians alike, for an ulterior motive: the practical goal of fulfilling the Great Commission. People tended to become means for us to achieve our ministry objectives, because our lives were dominated and motivated by an activist cause.

This activism turned me, in effect, into a manipulator of people. It was bad enough that I felt manipulated by my fellow Crusaders, but it hurt me more that I had begun to manipulate others. People had applied subtle pressure on me to become involved, and as I sought my own disciples, I put pressure on others. I was spurred on by the praise and recognition awarded to those with successful ministries.

In short, my life had become identified with a cause, and my participation in this cause was my primary source of satisfaction. It would require Catholic spirituality, with its emphasis on the path of humility and on the performing of quiet deeds of mercy and charity, to begin uprooting these tendencies from my heart.

One might wonder what became of the personal relationship with Christ so tirelessly preached by Evangelicals. Certainly Crusaders emphasized the importance of this relationship, but in my experience their practical orientation limited its development.

Scripture became a tool to be controlled by the reader to develop his character and increase his ministry. Absent was the Catholic understanding that through receptive and loving meditation on Scripture, Christ is conceived in our souls and begotten into the world through deeds of love. Even our praising of God was strictly active, as we looked for attributes of God in Scripture primarily to strengthen ourselves for ministry. Absent was the Catholic understanding of quiet, loving adoration.

As I slowly burned out from within, I began to dread the very idea of discipleship, and my Christian life became strained. I sought deeper roots in the Baptist church I had started attending, one of the finest Evangelical churches in my area. Unfortunately, this church could do little to help me regain a sound Christian life. The simple reason was that its spirituality differed little from the Crusade's.

It really should not have surprised me that this church should have the same orientation as the Crusade. After all, Evangelicals define themselves as Christians committed to the spread of the gospel. Their singing and other activities at Sunday services are structured primarily to encourage enthusiasm in the congregants (and to evangelize non-Christians). Their defining characteristic and reason for existence is commitment to a particular cause. This was shown vividly during a talk I attended given by a professor from Talbot Seminary. He explained that we were put on earth not to learn to worship God—after all, he said, we will worship God better when we see him face to face in heaven—but to evangelize.

Both the Crusade and contemporary Evangelicalism are descended in part from nineteenth century revivalism, a hallmark of which was the belief that excitement is necessary to revive and to spread the true religion. Often Evangelical church services are conducted as if they were designed for entertainment: There is never any dead time, and the congregation is fed songs, novel prayers, and preaching, with no opportunity for contemplative prayer.

Catholicism, by contrast, subordinates all causes to worship. The summit of the Christian life within Catholicism is the public worship of God in the liturgy, in union with the worship of God in heaven by the angels and saints. There is an essential continuity between our lives in heaven and on earth. This liturgical worship begins in receptivity—that is, in contemplation, which is nothing other than loving receptivity to God—and ends in sacrifice as we offer ourselves to God after receiving him deeper into our lives through the Eucharist.

This worship overflows into all of life, even the most active life, for even the most active life is subordinate to contemplative and sacrificial worship. From this overflow, all of our activity is elevated to worship insofar as we become living sacrifices to God, as expressed through our deeds of love. Evangelism is one form of these good deeds, an act of mercy nourished by worship as we draw others through their repentance and conversion into the true worship and adoration of God. Through the examples of Catholic saints such as Dominic and Catherine of Siena, I have been filled with a new desire for the salvation of souls. But Dominic in particular has shown me how to evangelize in accordance with my own abilities and personality—through my love of learning—rather than in accordance with the unsatisfactory model of the Campus Crusade.

Thus for me the greatest benefit of Catholicism has been the restoration of a deep relationship with Christ. Contrary to popular opinion, Catholic thinkers such as Thomas Aquinas have always understood the need for a personal relationship with Christ, although they have described that relationship in terms other than "personal." (After all, even enemies can know each other personally.) They explained instead that by justification we are made friends and lovers of God, and they understood what it meant to be a friend and lover of God better than any Evangelical I had ever encountered.

I learned from Bernard of Clairvaux and Catherine of Siena that the most fundamental form of prayer is the loving adoration of God, a prayer which exceeds the ability of words to express it. Whereas Evangelicals often think of the Spirit-filled life as one in which the Spirit controls us, Catholic writers teach that being Spirit-filled means that, as we meditate on and contemplate Christ and the Trinity, the Spirit inflames our hearts with love, and thus we willingly obey God.

In short, I found through my studies that the medieval Catholic focus on our relationship with Jesus could be summed up in these words of Thomas Aquinas: "I long for you to be in the heart of Jesus Christ, i.e., that you may love him intimately, and that you may be loved by him; for man's life consists in this" (*Commentary on Saint Paul's First Letter to the Thessalonians*).

Evangelicals often speak of a relationship with God based on the gratitude felt when they realize that God loves the unlovable. As a Catholic, my gratitude and love for God has deepened as I've learned that God by his grace goes even further and *makes* us lovable in his sight. It is commonplace among Catholic writers to note that God by grace beautifies the soul, adorning it with virtues. He does not leave us hateful to him, as Calvin taught, but dignifies us by enabling us through the grace of the indwelling Spirit of Christ to become worthy of eternal life (see Galatians 6:6-10 and Colossians 3:23-24).

The two aspects of Catholicism which Evangelicals most often claim are a hindrance to a personal relationship with Christ, ritual and hierarchy, have become for me a tremendous help in developing that relationship. The sacrament of the Eucharist has created in me a deep awareness of my dependence on the grace of God. Genuflecting at Mass moves me to bow before Christ's authority in all areas of my life, an experience which reflects the Catholic principle that bodily acts can influence the soul's disposition.

The hierarchical elements of the Church have helped me to draw nearer to Christ. Going to confession humbles me and helps uproot sinful tendencies from my heart. Obedience to the teachings and authority of the bishops and the pope has helped free me from bondage to my own interpretations as the measure of truth. I believe my capacity to receive Christ has been deepened through this obedience. After all, Jesus said that whoever receives his messengers receives him (Matt. 10:40).

Even though I value these spiritual benefits more than any other benefit, it was my intellectual struggles that completed my burnout and thus freed me to turn toward Catholicism. Here, again, Schaeffer had given me high expectations for Christianity. In his book *He is There and He is Not Silent*, Schaeffer wrote that Christianity is true not only to what Scripture says but true also to reality. A person can follow Christianity without ever having to fall off the end of the world intellectually. I soon suspected that Evangelical Christianity could not fulfill these expectations.

My difficulties began once again in the Campus Crusade. As I shared my faith with other college students, intellectual objections to Christianity were hurled at me. Convinced that Christianity was not an irrational religion, I strove to find answers. I consulted commentaries and the writings of various Evangelicals to find solutions. Gradually, I began to find these answers inadequate and became disillusioned with Evangelical thought, wondering if my relationship with Christ was being maintained at the expense of truth.

The first category of intellectual difficulties comprised biblical passages that conflicted with Evangelical theology. For example, in preaching that we were justified by faith alone, I often encountered the objection that James, in the second chapter of his epistle, clearly states that we are *not* justified by faith alone.

Evangelical commentators offered explanations of how this passage could agree with the Protestant interpretation of Paul's doctrine of justification, I never found these interpretations satisfactory. I had the uneasy feeling that the passage was being explained away rather than truly explained.

Jesus clearly emphasized the role of works in salvation. And Paul never used the phrase "faith alone." In fact, the only time "faith alone" or "faith only" is used in Scripture is by James, and he conclusively rejects the concept: "You see that a man is justified by works and not by faith alone" (Jas. 2:24). Schaeffer's influence prevented me from finding a solution to this problem so long as I remained a committed Evangelical. It would take the Catholic exposition of Paul's writings—centered in passages such as Galatians 5:6, which teaches that it is not faith alone, but faith formed by love which saves us—to show me the profound harmony between these two apostles.

Many other passages I encountered seemed to conflict with the broad outline of Evangelical theology and spirituality. This left me with a feeling of unease, yet I was hopeful that by trying to be more objective I could develop a more accurate, biblical understanding. I was never able to do this while an Evangelical.

As I realized later, the narrow confines of Protestant theology had constricted my ability to penetrate deeply into the teachings of Scripture. Only after I began to read Catholic works, especially the Church Fathers and medieval writers, did Scripture start to make more sense to me. Catholic thought opened Scripture to me in a way that Evangelical thought never had. From my Bible study I knew many Bible verses, but their rich meanings typically eluded me. The truly decisive intellectual problem for me centered on the second pillar of Evangelicalism, the doctrine of *sola scriptura*, the Bible as the sole authority of faith and practice.

Several specific influences gradually wore away my belief in *sola scriptura*. First, in my Baptist days I became interested in evangelizing Catholics, even acquiring materials from the Mission to Catholics for this purpose. Seeking to find and expose the errors in the Catholic view of tradition and Church authority, I studied passages of Scripture used by Evangelicals in their polemics against the Church. Ultimately I found these arguments wanting.

Evangelicals often argue, for example, that the injunction in Revelation 22:18-19 against adding anything to the "words of the prophecy of this book" secured *sola scriptura* and precluded Catholic tradition. But this "book of prophecy" refers only to the book of Revelation which was written as an individual book, not as the last section of an already compiled New Testament.

Furthermore, I encountered passages of Scripture that positively suggested the Catholic view. In John 16:13-15, Jesus tells his apostles that the Spirit will guide them into "all the truth." This presented a dilemma for me. If we allowed that this promise extended beyond the eleven apostles then present, the Catholic understanding of Tradition and the infallibility of the Magisterium would become reasonable. If the promise applied only to those present and to no one else, then many of the New Testament writers, such as Paul, could not have written under the inspiration of the Holy Spirit.

One could reply that the original apostles could pass on the grace of this spiritual guidance to others, but this implies successors to the apostles—and that is precisely the Catholic position.

It is not enough to say, as some Evangelicals do, that the apostles, such as Peter, merely approved what non-apostles, such as

Mark, had written. If Mark's Gospel was only "approved" by Peter, then that Gospel is only accurate, not inspired. Furthermore, the Evangelical argument concedes that it required the authority of the Church, with the apostles as its spokesmen, to recognize what writings were inspired and therefore to be included in the canon of Scripture.

The challenge of secularism and atheism, from which Christianity had originally rescued me, still haunted me. I decided as I finished my studies in English to pursue a second major in philosophy, hoping to work through the philosophical challenges I had encountered while evangelizing. My studies began with epistemology, the study of how we can have knowledge at all.

Exposed to the scourges of positivism and empiricism, philosophies that challenge the possibility of any rational knowledge of God, I sought a foundation for response in the thought of Carl F. H. Henry, a leading Evangelical thinker. He did not help much. Conceding important ground to empiricism, he argues that reason cannot prove the existence of God and that, instead, all theology must be based on a single presupposition: the living God revealed in his Word. Henry presupposes the truth of Evangelical Christianity and proceeds to show the flaws of every other system of thought.

This circular reasoning not only failed to convince me, but it also showed the impoverishment of *sola scriptura*. Henry claims his theory of knowledge is the biblical view, but in fact it stems from post-Cartesian philosophy. It became apparent to me that, in practice, even Evangelicals do not follow *sola scriptura*.

I had some familiarity with the historical defense of the authority of Scripture proposed by John Warwick Montgomery, an important Evangelical theologian opposed to presuppositionalism. In his view, we become convinced by historical evidence that Christ is the Son of God and that Christ spoke of the inspiration and authority of Scripture. This historical approach seemed to support Catholicism rather than Evangelicalism, since the canon of Scripture could be determined neither from Christ's explicit teachings nor from Scripture alone: The guidance of the Church was also necessary.

In the next phase of my studies I began investigating the thought of philosophers such as Aristotle, Plato, Hegel, and Heidegger. These writers exhibited a depth of thought I never had found as an Evangelical. Although I could not give up my love for Christ, I found myself being taken captive by philosophy. Two parallel processes began. Influenced by German idealism, I began to move in the direction of the liberal, experience-based theology that originated with Schleiermacher in the nineteenth century. In this approach, theology is essentially a reflection of personal experience.

At the same time, while doing research for my master's thesis, I began studying the writings of the Church Fathers and of medieval theologians and mystics. I was struck by the sublimity of their reflections on the Incarnation and the Trinity. These doctrines, or rather the realities they express, were an integral part of Catholic spirituality. They were not simply doctrines that had to be reluctantly defended, not intellectual liabilities. Yet even while I fell in love with these central Christian truths, my love was undermined by the man-centered spirituality of the liberal theology I had embraced.

The beginning of my liberation from such man-centered spirituality came through Catholic thinkers such as Augustine and Aquinas, who had confronted philosophy and transformed it in the light of Christian revelation rather than retreating into an anti-intellectual ghetto. In doing this they were following the example of the apostle Paul, who exhorted us to bring every thought captive to Christ and who in his own preaching, as in Acts 17:28 and his epistle to the Colossians, made use of Greek thought to communicate the gospel. This philosophical tradition helped me to rediscover the reasonableness of the Christian faith and thus fulfilled the expectations raised by Schaeffer.

The final moment of my liberation came with my discovery of Thomist realism, an alternative to empiricism and idealism. In studying the thought of Thomist philosophers such as Jacques Maritain and Etienne Gilson, I discovered that unlike empiricism, realism allows us to reach beyond our sense impressions in order to arrive at a natural knowledge of God. And unlike idealism, which keeps us locked in the prison of our own mind, realism allows us to be docile and receptive to reality outside ourselves. The receptivity of Catholic philosophy fully supports the receptivity of genuine Christian spirituality, and thus Catholic philosophy and spirituality, I found, form an integral unity.

Twelve years ago my spiritual and intellectual journey led me to enter the Catholic Church, where I discovered the true and highest spirituality. I have found since that there is no limit to the depth of the loving relationship we can have with Christ, a relationship that allows us to live in accord with reality, truth, and rationality. I have still only begun to explore the riches of Catholic spirituality, theology, and philosophy. In finding Catholicism I have found Christ—in a more profound way than ever before in my Christian experience.

# 7

# Out of the Frying Pan, Into the Fire

## *Sally Box*

In early 1985 I confided to a good friend that I had decided to enter the Catholic Church.

"Oh, Sally," she sighed, "Out of the frying pan, into the fire, right?"

I thought this an apt description, for I was leaving the almost-got-it-right Catholicism of the high-church Episcopalians for the fullness of faith to be found only in the Catholic Church.

I was brought up as an Episcopalian, and my early religious memories are of candles, vestments, the passing of the liturgical year, and services as near to the Divine Office and the Mass as you can get in a Protestant setting.

But from early childhood on, specifically Catholic things, like a sea-shell grotto on a lawn, a crucifix on the wall of a neighbor's home, or a classmate making the sign of the cross over her lunch, caught my attention and resonated in my consciousness.

My serious interest in the Catholic Church stems from a Girl Scout trip to New Mexico during which, to save time and trouble, we were all bundled off to Mass on Sunday evening. In Gallup, in 1966, the Mass was still celebrated in Latin. It was a mysterious and intriguing experience. The English translation in the pew missalette was reassuringly familiar and seemed a close cousin to the *Book of Common Prayer*. I did not realize then that the *Book of Common Prayer* was derived from the Mass, but it was an intriguing link.

Three things stay with me vividly from that evening. One was the strong sense of something special being in that church. Another was that the altar boy was wearing black high-top Keds under his cassock, not the spit-shined loafers I was used to. The third thing was the puzzling reaction of a good friend, a staunch Presbyterian, who sat through the Mass in rigid, Calvinistic disapproval. The "something special," I learned later, was the Real Presence. The server's Keds have come to symbolize for me the Church's ability to wed the sublime and the mundane. As for my friend's reaction: It was my first intimation that not everyone thinks the Catholic Church is the greatest.

My interest in Catholicism continued to grow during the next several years, although I did nothing directly about it. Encountering the Church and its influence on Western civilization through literature, art, and history in school, especially when reading Dante and Chaucer, I found much that was spiritually attractive. The idea that whole societies were once shaped by a Christian philosophy was fascinating. And when I spent a summer in Mexico as a high-school student, the unselfconscious piety of the people whose faith colored every aspect of their daily life appealed to me.

In the early 1970s I came across two engrossing novels. *In This House of Brede*, by Rumer Godden, is a moving story of enclosed monastic life and the struggles and joys of that religious vocation as lived out by a community of vivid and very human nuns. *The Cardinal*, by Henry Morton Robinson, is a sprawling saga of an Irish-American prelate's service to the Church in the early part of the twentieth century. It was not outstanding literature, but its account of Catholic life in all its variety, from family home to poor rural parish to the halls of the Vatican, was compellingly attractive, partly because the Church seemed so frank about the human frailties of its members.

The books inspired me to attend Mass at the local campus church, where I was in for a severe shock. The promulgation of the New Rite of the Mass was still in its early and experimental stages in 1972, and the difference between what I expected, based on my previous experiences and my reading, and what I saw at the Mass, was glaring and disheartening. The sense of the other that I had had years ago was missing, as was the Latin, the meditative silence, and the mystery. At nineteen, I wasn't able to make the necessary distinctions between substance and accidents where the liturgy was concerned, and I was so discouraged that I gave up further exploration. I didn't enter a Catholic church again for another six years.

During this time I was sidetracked in my journey toward the Catholic Church in part because I had come across the high-church faction of the Episcopal tradition, which has a style of practice and theology that, in many ways, closely resembles what I thought of as traditional Catholicism. Though I had been a practicing Episcopalian all my life, this was a new discovery for me.

By the purest serendipity, in Advent of 1974 I encountered St. Francis Episcopal Church and the Rev. Homer Rogers. A strong believer in the parochial system, I was simply looking for the Episcopal church closest to our new apartment. But I fell into a remarkable parish. It was quite a small group, mostly because of its blend of strict adherence to what we understood to be orthodox Christianity and a heavy high-church liturgical tradition, which is not for the spiritually faint of heart.

What made the parish unique was its strong community life which pursued two goals concurrently: the worship of God and the making of saints. The whys and wherefores of these goals were constantly explained and illustrated by the pastor. Fr. Rogers, who died in 1980, was an outstanding apologist whose sermons, parish letters, and nine-month-long instruction courses were master-pieces of Christian education. Listening to him was a Eureka! experience in which things vaguely known or suspected were made vividly clear.

Though I realize now that because of his denominational limits, many of his explanations could go only so far, and no further before crossing the boundary into Roman Catholicism yet I owe a great debt of gratitude to his instruction in classical Christianity.

I was taken with the warmth and friendliness of the parish and with the idea of an "Episcopal" Catholicism. It seemed to supply not just an active, intellectual understanding of Christianity but also the most attractive part of Catholic liturgy and devotion—without the disciplinary difficulties of actually joining Rome. High-church Episcopalians are fully convinced they are a valid branch of Catholic Christianity, sharing the apostolic faith, the seven sacraments, and apostolic succession with the Roman and Orthodox churches. They are the "smells and bells" segment of the Episcopal church, going in for incense, statues, holy water, the stations of the cross, and other sacramentals. Most high-church Episcopalians have an excellent understanding of the communion of saints, and many of them have a deep Marian devotion.

The high-church Episcopalian option also got me out of a potentially unpleasant dilemma by allowing me to shelve any decision on the Catholic Church's claim to have the fullness of faith, since I was able to enjoy so many Catholic practices within Episcopalianism.

My husband had strong opinions about the Catholic Church, few of them favorable, and he had made it plain that being married to a Catholic was not something he could contemplate with enthusiasm. It was a relief to drop the subject for a while and to immerse myself in the life of the parish, where I served in the Altar Guild and taught Sunday school.

I had many good reasons for wanting high-church Episcopalianism to work, but as time passed, there arose many questions about its validity that I could not answer satisfactorily. I began to wonder why, if we were so Catholic, no one else seemed to know it but us. Our position began to remind me of that of a self-proclaimed sovereign state that is recognized by itself but not by any other country. Sometimes I saw us as a little brother tagging along after the big guys, the Roman Catholic Church and the Orthodox churches. Granted, a thing can be true even if its truth is not widely known. But if we were really part of what we called "Catholic Christendom," why did this need constant reiteration among ourselves? Was somebody protesting too much? Our inability to leave the subject alone suggested that we might not be as sure as we'd like.

Several Catholic doctrines, which we as Episcopalians had jettisoned, made sense to me. Take, for example, the papacy. The Scripture passages used to explain the primacy of Peter, a doctrine discounted by Episcopalians, seemed clear and understandable. I remember listening to a tape of a Protestant minister who was explaining in annoyed detail why Matthew 16:18 couldn't possibly mean that Peter was "the rock" because two different Greek words were used for the term. I'd had enough Latin and Greek to recognize the fallacy in his argument: You don't use a feminine noun like *petra* to refer to a man, like Simon. You use a masculine form of the word, hence *Petros*.

But it was the vehemence of his argument that puzzled me. If the papacy didn't affect him, why did he care? Why, instead of promoting what their own denominations taught, did so much of Protestant apologetics concern itself with refuting Catholic doctrine?

Being in the Episcopal church with its internal disputes and its falling away into secularism, and looking across to Rome was like looking into a mirror, but with one big difference. In Rome, the buck stops someplace, and that place is with the pope. A case in point: The Episcopal Church USA voted to ordain women in 1976 and, later, to consecrate them as bishops. Faced with pressure to do the same, the pope said no, and said that the matter was closed for discussion.

It didn't seem reasonable to me that God, knowing human nature, would set up an organization without providing it with some sort of unmistakable, visible leadership. It also didn't seem reasonable that Christianity had been in error about this leadership for fifteen hundred years until the Reformation.

The history of the Catholic Church had to be considered. Its adamant presence from the descent of the Holy Spirit onward— not always strong or wisely administered, but there without a break—was a fact that was hard to ignore. The counter-argument was that a united Christendom under the papacy was both a Roman exaggeration and a political expedient, and that the Anglican church had always been a separate entity with its own bishops prior to the arrival in 596 of Augustine of Canterbury. But this would not hold up. The existence of the Sarum Rite, unique to England, and the insularity and independent spirit of the English church were cited as well. But, try as I might, I couldn't imagine Pre-Reformation English saints like Anselm, Augustine, Hilda,

Hugh, or the Venerable Bede considering themselves Anglicans. There is an English Catholic tradition, just as there is a French and a Spanish and a German tradition, but it was Catholic first and English second.

Each time I weighed the Catholic account of history or doctrine against the Episcopal version, the Catholic version tipped the scales. Catholic history, even when learned from secular sources, fit the facts more accurately. The explication of doctrine was fuller and richer, because none of it had had to be trimmed to fit post-Reformation concepts.

On an intellectual level I was making progress, but on a practical level I was disappointed in the Catholics, lay and clerical, whom I encountered. They didn't seem very Catholic to me. They seemed embarrassed that anyone might think they actually believed certain things the Church taught. They seemed eager to distance themselves from former traditions and practices. The enthusiasm of my Episcopalian friends for being what they considered Catholic stood out in marked contrast and, in spite of my theological doubts, it still exerted a great influence on me.

I attended a Catholic instruction class in 1977. It was taught by nuns wearing pantsuits and using as their text the deficient *Christ Among Us*. The discussions centered on why the Church made everyone's life so tough. My disillusionment that everyone in the Church was not behaving like the good examples in the Baltimore Catechism seems childish now, but it gave me an excuse to stay away for another seven years.

These were years spent becoming even more convinced of the truth of Catholic claims. The credit for this goes to the Holy Spirit, of course, but also to the owner of the local Catholic bookstore, who kept me supplied with orthodox and worthwhile books and periodicals and was always available to discuss the Church.

From acquaintances I made there and through my reading, I discovered that although the current face of the Church might not resemble my vision, there were still many who were loyal to the Magisterium, refusing to compromise the faith, and I longed to be one of them.

It finally dawned on me that I alone would be responsible for the type of Catholic I would be. Others in the Church could help or hinder me, but I would be accountable for my own actions. In the end, I came to understand that my dissatisfaction with other Catholics, the sorry state (to Episcopalian eyes and ears) of the Catholic liturgy, and even the probable conflict I would have within my own family were mere difficulties—but they were not doubts. And only honest doubt can excuse someone from being obedient to the express wish of our Lord that "all may be one."

I realize now that I didn't really need my husband's permission to become a Catholic, but I did want it. Once I had it, grudgingly given, I entered the Church at breakneck speed. My sponsor, the bookstore owner, directed me to a priest who himself was a former Episcopalian.

After my conversion, I ran across passages in Caryll Houselander's *The Dry Wood* in which she draws a contrast between the "Aunthood" of the Church of England and "the Catholic Church, with her celibate clergy, her virgin heart, her disconcerting vulgarity, and the riffraff of the whole world clinging to her flamboyant skirts . . . unquestionably the Universal Mother." That sums it up. The Episcopal church was fine, so far as it went; it just didn't go far enough.

If I had to choose one word to define being a Catholic, it would be "more." There is more faith, but more aggravation; more hope, but more pain; more joy, but more sorrow; more of everything. I attribute this heightened sense to being immersed in the real thing rather than in a sincere but pale imitation; to being embraced by the Mother instead of the Aunt; to being out of the frying pan and into the fire of God's love.

# 8

# Converted by Mozart

## *Eric M. Johnson*

Almost every Sunday of my life I have gone to church. But only recently did I discover the real reason for going.

Some of my first memories are of the Chapel of Cornelius the Centurion on Governor's Island, New York, the Coast Guard base where my family lived. We moved to Virginia when I was five, and I grew up attending a Lutheran church a few miles from our home.

My mother interspersed religious with secular stories when she read to my brother and me. We particularly loved C. S. Lewis's *Chronicles of Narnia* and Old Testament stories from an illustrated children's Bible: stories of men fighting, walls tumbling, and seas parting at the stroke of a staff.

Although my father was raised a Mormon, he had not practiced that faith since before I was born. He directed our church's choir but stayed seated when it came time for communion. He never talked about religion, and during our family prayer time he remained silent. I remember wanting him to pray. I even asked him to, but he refused.

Our Lutheran church services went strictly by the book. As an acolyte I knew that we were performing a ritual, not showing off. No one ever thought to alter or paraphrase the words of a prayer, or to insert a personal message into the liturgy, or to refrain from kneeling at the altar rail when receiving communion. As a child, I thought church was deadly boring, but I did not attribute that to the unchanging nature of the liturgy.

There was an unspoken stigma attached to anyone who got too excited about God. Our pastor's daughter once remarked, "We believe what Catholics do, we're just not as loud about it." Of course, that wasn't exactly true—there were huge differences between the two churches—but her statement epitomized a problem in mainline Protestantism.

Not that I wanted to preach the gospel. I wanted to play baseball and video games. My report cards usually had a note from the teacher that began, "Eric has a lot of potential, but. . . ." I was always finding activities that had nothing to do with schoolwork. Had I been born ten years later I might have been diagnosed with attention deficit disorder. My father diagnosed my behavior as rank laziness, and he was right. With parents of different faiths, a lukewarm church, and a naturally unruly disposition, I was headed toward religious indifference.

During those early years my knowledge of Catholicism was murky. My Sunday school education taught me that Lutherans were fortunate not to be forced to worship statues, that we could read the Bible without a priest looking over our shoulders, and that we did not need the pope to tell us what to do. History classes affirmed that Catholic efforts during the Counter-Reformation, particularly through the Council of Trent, stunted the expansion of Protestantism.

In high school—a period of adolescent rebellion during which I smoked cigars, listened to classical music, grew long hair, and engaged in conservative politics—my brushes with Catholicism were infrequent, but my brushes with Catholics were constant. Most of my friends were "papists," which I was generous enough to overlook. Occasionally I would accompany them to Mass at the local Catholic parish. The music was middlebrow schmaltz, a distinct contrast to the stately Lutheran hymns I had grown up with. Often a member of the Catholic folk group would play a banjo solo during the conclusion of the Eucharistic prayer. At other times, a pianist would play while singing into a microphone suspended near his mouth. It was so much like a lounge act, I half-expected to see a tip jar on the piano.

There were other, more serious problems with this local parish that kept me away from the Catholic Church for a long time. But I also saw glimpses of deeper, more enduring aspects of Catholicism. I observed in many of my friends' families a closeness and vitality that I could not help but attribute to their faith. Now and then, when reading a newspaper or magazine, I would come across some bit of a papal pronouncement or papal encyclical, and, though I did not grasp their full meaning, their breadth and solidity impressed me. At bottom, I knew that the Church stood for certain things and did not back down, no matter how much the world raged against it. That made a powerful impression on a young man struggling toward adulthood.

After I entered college my contact with formal religion was limited to Sunday services at a Presbyterian church that I attended with my girlfriend, Paige. Were it not for a sense of obligation, I probably would have fallen away from active churchgoing altogether.

It was through music and art that I first encountered a positive, inspiring vision of Catholicism. In fact, when people ask me today about my conversion, I often tell them I was converted by Mozart. That's an exaggeration, but not far from the truth. To be young is to be a sensualist, and it was through my ears and eyes that I first became attracted to the faith.

I was seventeen when my parents ordered a compact disc of Gregorian chant from a music club. As a choir director, my father was always looking for new material, but I don't think he could have possibly considered this for the choir. Perhaps they received the recording by accident and kept it. Whatever the reason, I listened to it often, intrigued by the otherworldly stillness it brought to my soul. My reservations about the Catholic Church softened as I listened to it. No institution that nurtured such beauty could be all bad.

That insight deepened as my musical tastes expanded and my appreciation for Catholic composers grew. The repertoire of the madrigal singing group in my senior year of high school included choral staples such as Mozart's *Ave Verum Corpus* and *Lacrimosa*. Until I encountered these works, I had little appreciation for the majesty of God. Mozart may not have been the most exemplary Catholic, but that didn't bother me much. He said that when he composed he found nothing more inspirational than the words "Lamb of God, who takest away the sin of the world, have mercy on us." Such sinners who seek forgiveness will never hear an unkind word from me. I marvel at their humility.

But it was a lesser known Renaissance composer who provided me with the most dramatic fusion of fidelity and musical strength. My friend Steve who was majoring in music education, always played his latest acquisitions for me. "Listen to this disc I just bought," he said. From the opening notes, I thought I was hearing a modern choral piece, but it turned out to be four centuries old. It was a forty-part motet titled *Spem in Alium*. It lasts nine minutes, although its text is only thirty-one words long, and it pulsates with the hidden pain of a man who remained steadfast while he watched his faith being destroyed in his country. The words are:

*Spem in alium nunquam habui*
*praeter in te, Deus Israel,*
*qui irasceris et propitius eris,*
*et omnia peccata hominum*
*in tribulatione dimittis.*
*Domine Deus,*
*creator coeli et terrae,*
*respice humilitatem nostram.*

I have never founded my hope
on any other than thee, O God of Israel,
who shalt be angry and yet be gracious,
and who absolvest all the sins of mankind
in tribulation.
Lord God,
creator of heaven and earth,
be mindful of our lowliness.

I became transfixed by the consummate beauty of the work, as well as by its intricate complexity. The composer was Thomas Tallis (1505–1585), who conducted the choir of the Chapel Royal—the summit of all choral positions in sixteenth century England—and wrote music for various feasts and events. Tallis remained Catholic even under the persecution of Queen Elizabeth, a time when going to Mass incurred a substantial fine and being a priest could mean a visit with the executioner.

The visual arts also drew me to Catholicism. It is impossible to survey the history of art without running into the fact that a huge number of great works were created for the glory of God. The vast majority of those works, whether they were paintings or cathedrals, were created by Catholics.

A trip to Europe just prior to the start of college had revealed to me something about the difference between Catholic and Protestant art. Four of my classmates and I visited a late Gothic church in Salzburg: its interior was a blank, gleaming white. We had toured enough churches by then for me to notice what was missing: no statues in the niches, no reliefs carved on the altar, no religious scenes over the apse, no stations of the cross. A tour book noted that the church had become Protestant early in the Reformation, and the parishioners had razed everything that smacked of "popery" and had whitewashed the great paintings on the walls.

By contrast, when we went to Rome and I entered St. Peter's Basilica, my Protestant sensibilities were shocked by what I regarded as gaudy ornamentation and distastefully expensive decorations. (I have returned there since my conversion, and it all looks perfectly appropriate now. In fact, compared to many aristocratic palaces, it is positively austere.) My friends and I split up to explore the massive basilica, and as I walked to the right, intending to wind my way toward the main altar, I found myself facing Michelangelo's *Pietà*.

Reproductions I had come across in previous years had made me admire the skill of the Florentine sculptor, but I was unprepared for the impact of beholding the *Pietà* in person. Mary's sorrow in holding her dead son is poignant yet bereft of despair;

her countenance is suffused with divine radiance as she contemplates the innocent Victim.

Bustling sounds behind me melted into oblivion as I sank to my knees. Tears streamed down my face as I studied the sculpted flesh of Christ and marveled at the dexterity and the depth of soul necessary to produce such a wonder.

It was both an increasing intellectual crisis and a growing aesthetic appreciation of Christian art that forced me to consider the claims of Jesus Christ for the first time. I had attended church all those years, but I had never asked some basic questions: Who is God? What does he want from me? Does believing in Jesus matter?

I began reading apologetics, especially the books of C. S. Lewis. I saw that the case for Christianity does not rest so much on one irrefutable line of reasoning but on a thousand probabilities that add up to one great certainty.

One the most compelling arguments I encountered was based on the fact that Jesus Christ claimed to be God and that his statement must be either true or false. If it is false, Jesus either deliberately deceived his followers, in which case he was a liar, or he unknowingly deceived his followers, in which case he was a lunatic. But knowing what we do about human nature, Jesus acted like neither a lunatic nor a liar. His words and deeds showed no sign of dementia. It is even less likely that he was a liar because his lies got him nothing except a slow, bloody death. The remaining possibility—that he claimed to be God because he really was God—fit the facts most closely.

After devouring as many books as I could on Christianity, I suddenly *understood*. The sense overtook me as I walked to my car one day. A moment before, it all looked so confusing, but then all at once the reality of the gospel permeated my mind. I wanted to place God first in my life, not simply pay lip service to him.

I began attending meetings of Evangelical groups on campus, especially Campus Crusade for Christ. It was largely through their influence, along with Paige's example, that I became a serious Christian.

But questions remained. I believed that the Old Testament foretold Christ's arrival; I believed Jesus was fully God and fully man,
was crucified for the forgiveness of our sins, and rose again to
show he had conquered death. I believed that the apostles spread
the good news just as it says in the book of Acts. What happened
next is a matter of some dispute in Christianity, and it was the historical agnosticism among Evangelicals that I found most trou-
bling. I was getting my degree in history, and my inclination to
ask, "What about the next two thousand years?" was becoming
overwhelming.

As near as I could tell, the only game in town until the Reformation was Catholicism. I began to read general histories of
Christianity. During spring break, confined to bed because of
minor surgery on my foot, I began to read through several issues
of *This Rock*, a magazine that a friend had given me. At first, I
simply liked the novelty of reading something from the opposite
point of view, but, despite my combative nature, I started to admire
the strong and fair-minded material. I began to find it enticing. I
could see where one teaching rested on another and how
doctrines interlocked.

I also discovered that most of the things I thought I knew about
the Catholic Church were wrong. I found Catholic theology
richer, and the historical case for Catholicism stronger, than any
other. The phrase "Catholic Church" first occurs in the historical
record in the writing of Ignatius of Antioch, only seven decades
after the Resurrection. The term saw wide use after that, and the
ancient writers who used it appeared to know precisely what they
were referring to: not a vague, amorphous, invisible group of
believers, but a visible community led by bishops who taught in
the name of Christ and the apostles.

My haphazard Protestant education had taught me that things
like prayers for the dead, veneration of saints, and forgiveness of
sins by the mediation of a priest were later additions tacked onto
pure Christianity by the Catholic Church. But the writings of the
earliest Christians firmly contradicted this. The teachings were not
as developed as they are today, nor did the government of the

Church remain in the same form. But then one would expect to see a difference between a beleaguered little group of religious outlaws and the worldwide body of 1 billion believers into which the Church has grown.

Surveying the Church's 2,000-year record, I noticed another strange fact. No matter where it was, even under friendly governments and during peaceful times, the Church never quite managed to become respectable. Whenever a society thought it had domesticated the gospel, there would arise someone, a Francis of Assisi for instance, to shake the complacency of those who preferred to relax and enjoy their comforts rather than to serve others.

The contemporary example of Pope John Paul II was foremost in my mind. How tempting it could be to show up in a foreign country, soak up the adulation of the crowds, utter a few platitudes, and fly off in a cloud of ersatz goodwill. Here, however, was a man whose love for humanity was so great that he challenged whole nations to strive for a more perfect order—and he risked opprobrium for doing so. The sight of a leader who neither pandered to our worst impulses nor consulted opinion polls to mold his message was deeply impressive to me.

Was the pope the head of the one, true Church of Christ? After all, there are a lot of churches out there. How can anyone say that a particular church is the right one? And doesn't that mean the other Christians are wrong? The answer, say Catholics, is that most of what the other churches teach is true but incomplete. What is missing is a coherent explanation of how God works in the world. God took on human flesh to be a living sacrifice for us and to teach us by word and example. He underwent not only physical pain of death by torture, but also mental anguish as he paid for every sin that ever was and ever will be committed. Was it really so implausible, I reasoned, that the Lord would fashion an instrument to preserve the memory of Jesus' words and deeds and that he would protect that memory from corruption? And if he wished to convey his saving grace through baptism, why wouldn't Jesus anoint leaders to direct that mission? God instituted two sacred priesthoods in the Old Testament: Why couldn't he have instituted one in the New?

If the Catholic Church were not the true Church, then it was a horrible monstrosity because it presumed to speak with the authority of God but it taught erroneously. Would a God of justice permit his name to be misused in this way for fifteen centuries prior to the Reformation?

Pondering all of this again one day, I suddenly put down the Catholic book I was reading. "My God," I thought. "I actually believe this stuff."

It seemed that in my heart I had become a Catholic. I couldn't have been more surprised if I had become a salamander. The truth was that I didn't *want* to be Catholic. It would disrupt my life. But I knew in the end that I had to have the courage of my convictions and follow through on my new beliefs. I know others who experienced profound joy when they reached that point, but for me the joy would be delayed.

Paige and I had once agreed that we should "take a look at Catholicism"—as if we were going to take a look at a car in a showroom. But this change in me came as a complete surprise. The night I told her I was converting to Catholicism, she cried.

"You know we can't get married now," she said. I told her that I had known she would be upset and assured her that we should continue to see each other. I urged her to consider studying Catholicism and to open herself up to it.

My parents were stunned at the news. My mother, after telling me she was more shocked by my announcement than by anything else she had ever heard, insisted that I speak with the pastor of our family's church, which I agreed to do out of respect for her.

The two meetings I had with the pastor were odd for both of us. He had studied at Catholic University for his master's degree in medieval studies and knew more about Catholicism than I did. We talked elliptically about faith and belief and about how Christians are supposed to grow intellectually. At last he came to the point: Why was I doing this? My mother, he told me, thought it was for political reasons. Didn't I know that Catholicism does not

endorse political ideologies, and that I could be a Lutheran conservative without contradiction?

"Yes," I replied. "But my reasons are not political. I have come
to believe that the pope is the Vicar of Christ, and that we should
ask Mary and the saints to pray for us, and more."

"You certainly picked the big ones," he replied.

During the following months I exerted no pressure on Paige to
look at the Catholic faith, and I went out of my way to avoid anything that resembled coercion. I talked with her when she wanted
to know more about the Church, but I left the subject alone if it
didn't come up. She began attending confirmation class with me,
just to see what it was like, and then she started going to Mass
with me on Sundays.

There came a day when I noticed that Paige had been reading a
book on Catholicism. I asked if it was any good. She nodded
weakly.

"Are you Catholic?" I asked.

"No. And neither are you," she shot back.

"I'm not confirmed, but that doesn't mean I'm not Catholic."

"It all makes too much sense!" she exclaimed.

"Something can't make *too much* sense," I said. "Do you believe it?"

A pause, then finally, "Yes."

Paige and I are now married and have two small children. My
parents have reconciled themselves to our conversion and have
even attended Christmas and Easter Masses with us for the past
few years, as well as our son's and daughter's baptisms.

When we were confirmed in the Catholic student center of our
university at the Easter Vigil Mass in 1994, I expected to be overwhelmed by the experience and to feel all the weight of the new
responsibility I was taking on as a full member of the Church. But
when the priest dipped his thumb in the sacred oil and marked
the sign of the cross on my forehead, I felt I had been let in on an
exhilarating cosmic secret. After we returned to our seats, Paige
and I could not contain our mirth.

I suddenly understood why artists depict the saints with solemn
expressions. Earthly temptations come wearing pleasing faces but

prove to be empty inside. The things of God can look grim and stern on the outside, but when they are embraced they prove nourishing and satisfying beyond all expectations. I had discovered the secret smile hidden behind every saint's face.

# 9

# Why I Became a Catholic

## *Robert Ian Williams*

How could you do it? Were you really converted? Do you worship Mary now? How can you tell your innermost secrets to another man in confession? Do you really know Jesus Christ? Why did you convert? How can you accept teaching that is not in the Bible?

My entry into the Catholic Church was not a Damascus Road conversion. Although God can work like that, my journey to the historic faith was a gradual learning experience. Conversion is ultimately an act of God's surprising grace. In many ways the process for me was like a detective novel in which one is always confounded to discover who the real villain is. I thought the Catholic Church was the villain, but at the end of my journey all my conceptions were confounded and turned upside down.

My dissatisfaction with the confusion I found within Evangelical Christianity was a starting point. That I began to see the weaknesses of this system was due, I believe, to the grace of God. Before that dissatisfaction began, I had been perfectly happy with Evangelical Christianity. I had trusted in Christ, believed my sins were forgiven, and thought I knew the gospel of the New Testament.

As for other religions, I thought they were all wrong. More particularly, I saw the Catholic Church as an apostate church, full of medieval corruption, obscuring the gospel and leading souls astray. I was convinced that the Word of God found in the Bible was the sole authority for the believer (*sola scriptura*) and that I was justified by faith alone (*sola fide*). These were the two rallying cries of the Reformation. When I met Catholics, I tried to show them the truth and lead them to a knowledge of the Lord. I was so anti-Catholic that I refused to pray in an Evangelical prayer meeting at my university because it was held in the Catholic chaplaincy. Because I knew that the Evangelical Christian Union sought the conversion of Catholics, I thought this arrangement plain hypocrisy.

Little did I know it but God's grace was beginning to work in my heart. It began over the issue of baptism. Evangelical Christians are sharply divided between those who accept infant baptism and those who believe baptism is for the adult believer only. I studied the facts and could find no explicit reference to infant baptism in the New Testament, so I decided to find out when this practice had entered Christianity. Could it be traced to the apostles, or did it creep in during the early centuries?

I found that the historical record endorsed infant baptism. If it had been an innovation, why was there no record in Church history of protest at its introduction? I could find no Christian group prior to the sixteenth century that had rejected infant baptism. Even after the Reformation, those first Baptist Christians only sprinkled the adult believer. Believers' baptism by immersion (also a matter of dispute among some Evangelicals) came about only in the seventeenth century. Baptist church histories, I found, were short on accuracy and continuity.

I therefore rejected adult-only baptism. To me this was a key area of truth, and I tried to convince Baptist Evangelicals of the error of their belief. I was told by some that I was becoming obsessed with a peripheral issue. This shocked me. How could a solemn command of Jesus Christ be regarded as peripheral?

I was amazed when I read what a renowned Evangelical leader, Martyn Lloyd-Jones, had to say in his book *What Is an Evangelical?* Commenting on Evangelical disunity, he states:

> Another matter we must put in the same category is the age and mode of baptism: the age of the candidate, and the mode of administering the rite of baptism. I would put that again into the non-essential category for the same reason, that you cannot prove one or the other from the Scriptures. I have been reading books on the subject for the last 44 years and more, and I know less about it now

than I did at the beginning. Therefore, while I assert, and we must all assert, that we believe in baptism, for that is plainly commanded, yet we must not divide and separate over the age of the candidate or over the mode of administration.

Here was a man who believed that the Bible was the only authority for the believer, and yet he could not establish the biblical pattern for baptism. It was truly a case of ever learning and never coming to the knowledge of the truth. Ironically, Lloyd-Jones in the same volume teaches the perspicuity of Scripture and that Evangelicalism is clearer in its thinking than Catholicism!

This suddenly focused in my mind the other disagreements among Evangelicals. If they, too, were peripheral, then why the separated denominations and the contending theories on the Lord's return, the meaning of the Lord's Supper, whether the believer could lose his salvation, and the question of charismatic gifts? The list could go on.

Even a conservative Evangelical such as Anglican John Stott manifested this subjective tendency when he decided to reject the idea of eternal punishment and to substitute for it annihilation. Yet the same John Stott (clearly going against the tide of 2,000 years of Christian exegesis and interpretation, which has affirmed the punishment of the wicked in hell) would turn in disdain to the gay lobby, which has "discovered" new meaning to the words of Paul on homosexuality! Such is the eclectic nature of the Protestant mind. John Stott and others may not realize it, but subjectivism and private judgment (the real hallmark of the Reformers) are ultimately the origin of theological liberalism.

Evangelicals complained about churchmen who recited the Nicene Creed and rejected the Christian belief in the resurrection of Jesus Christ, but at the same time they denied the clause "and I believe in one baptism for the remission of sins." They did so by claiming that the Creed's framers really meant this to be the baptism of the spirit in conversion, and not water baptism. As with the liberals, it was really a dishonest interpretation, and totally unhistorical. Every Christian figure prior to the sixteenth century believed that to be born again was to be baptized.

My academic training was as an historian, so I looked carefully and objectively at Church history. I was amazed that I could find no trace of Evangelical Christianity in the Church prior to the sixteenth century. Some of the groups posited by Evangelicals as proto-evangelicals, such as the Cathars and Montanists, were in reality heretical on such basic doctrine as the very nature of Christ. The followers of Wycliffe knew nothing of justification by faith alone, and the Waldensians, when they united with the Swiss reformers, had great difficulty in accepting it. Both groups participated in the sacraments of the Catholic Church and were originally reform movements, not churches.

Not one of the Church Fathers preached justification by faith alone. Wycliffe died hearing Mass, unbaptized as a believer, satisfied with his Catholic infant baptism! His followers, the Lollards, held a multiplicity of beliefs, many of which would be regarded by present-day Evangelicals as heretical. What Evangelical minister would uphold Wycliffe's principle of no payment for ministers, or his theory that property could be held only by righteous persons?

The theory that the acceptance of Christianity by the Roman Emperor Constantine in the fourth century had begun the corruption in the Church seemed even less credible. I found that the early Church leaders believed in infant baptismal regeneration, bishops, apostolic succession, the Real Presence of Christ in the Eucharist, a sacrificing priesthood, prayers for the dead, and the special role of the Bishop of Rome. All this could be found centuries prior to Constantine. In the words of Cardinal Newman, "He that studies history ceases to be a Protestant."

I could find no record of Evangelical Bible Christians, a faithful remnant clinging to the distinctive Evangelical tenets of Scripture alone and justification by faith alone. Evangelical treatment of Church history was superficial, and at its worst was simply a revision of history. The futility of such history-writing reminded me of the stepsisters in *Cinderella* trying to make the glass slipper fit. Such history speaks of men such as Ambrose, Augustine, and Athanasius as Bible-only Christians. But insofar as it ignores their evident Catholic context, it is intellectually dishonest. Augustine's view of justification and grace is in perfect harmony with Catholic teaching, but Evangelicals persist in appropriating him.

When I attempted to discuss this issue of continuity with fellow Evangelicals, they were dismissive. Their response seemed totally subjective. The evidence, they asserted, was lost to history (probably destroyed by the Catholics), but the internal witness of their conversion assured them that there must have been true Christians believing the Evangelical gospel down through the ages. This reminded me of the Mormon response to critics who ask for historical evidence for the *Book of Mormon*. Their answer is a similarly "spiritual" one, unsupported by historical or archaeological evidence.

What then was Evangelical history based on? I found that it was based on myths, myths not just about its continuity but also about the Catholic Church. I had been told the Catholic Church had burned copies of the Bible. I found that the Church had guarded the Bible, defined its canon, and had burned and forbidden the reading of editions that were inaccurate and heretical translations. Bibles such as Tyndale's translation had footnotes attacking the Church and the pope. I found that translations into vernacular languages had been made years before the Reformation. The Gospels had been translated into Anglo-Saxon long before the English language was formed.

I also found that the famous *Book of Martyrs* written by John Foxe, a sixteenth-century apostate Catholic, was historically inaccurate. Many of the "martyrs" in the reign of Mary Tudor were unorthodox and would have been burned in the reign of Protestant Queen Elizabeth. Indeed, Foxe supported a regime that tortured and killed Catholics who simply wanted to live in the faith of their ancestors. He also supported a regime that burned Evangelical Christians, such as those who rejected infant baptism! It was Protestant Christians who had persecuted the Puritan Pilgrim Fathers of seventeenth-century England, and the Pilgrims in their turn, on settling in America, had persecuted fellow Bible believers!

I had accepted the completely false idea perpetuated by Lloyd-Jones and other Evangelical teachers that Catholics believed in continuing revelation. On the contrary, I found that Catholic doctrine taught that public revelation ceased with the apostles and that the faith had been only once delivered to the saints. It was the duty of the Church as the pillar and foundation of the truth (1 Tim. 3:15) to discern and interpret that original deposit.

The Catholic Church, contrary to the myth, had not invented transubstantiation in the thirteenth century any more than it had invented the Trinity in the fourth. As an Evangelical I was perplexed to find myself in the same position as the Jehovah's Witness who says the word "Trinity" is not in the Bible. I would respond that the teaching was there and that the term simply defined it. Yet the Catholic could say the same to me about purgatory, and my response would have been that purgatory cannot be clearly seen. This would have been a weak reply, as Evangelicals are subjective as to what they see. After all, Luther, Calvin, Wesley, and a host of others could see infant baptism while Spurgeon, Billy Graham, and others could not.

The Catholic teaching was more logical. God had established a Church to be the final arbiter, and God is not the author of confusion. The development of doctrine, I came to think, is like the slow development of a photographic image. The image is on the film, but as time passes and conditions change, the image emerges more clearly.

I could not find one text that asserted that the Bible alone was sufficient. The famous passage that asserts that Scripture is profitable (2 Tim. 3:16) means, in fact, that it is helpful, not that it is sufficient. It is profitable for me to drink water for my health, but it is not sufficient. I could not find one verse that taught that the Word of God was purely the enscripturated. I found that Jesus had honored non-scriptural tradition in the Jewish faith community to which he belonged. His condemnation of the false interpretation of tradition given by the Pharisees was not a condemnation of tradition per se. The Church he founded on his apostles (Peter in particular) was a Church that accepted teaching both in written epistle and by word of mouth (2 Thess. 2:15).

I momentarily decided to re-examine my belief in Christ.

Could I be deluded? Was Jesus Christ in fact a false messiah? After all, the Jews reject him. Could the world's most brilliant and enduring people be wrong?

I read Jewish apologetical works against Christianity. They attacked the Christian faith by trying to show that the prophecies of the Hebrew Bible were not fulfilled and that the writers of the New Testament had altered the Old Testament texts. I discovered, however, that most Jewish polemical material was based on the writings of a Karaite scholar. The Karaites are a sect that was excommunicated from Judaism in the ninth century because they taught the authority of Scripture alone, rejecting rabbinical tradition. They failed to take into account that the writers of the New Testament wrote from a typically Jewish perception and redaction of the texts. Many Jewish polemicists claimed that Jesus never claimed divinity and that later Gentile followers had introduced "pagan concepts" such as the Virgin Birth and the Incarnation. This fascinated me, since there is much anti-Catholic material that claims that distinctive Catholic beliefs are pagan accretions. This is the Evangelical theory taken to its logical conclusion, and quite a few Evangelicals have abandoned Christianity along this route.

I was further challenged by one anti-Christian book that asked Christians this question: If Christ's religion is true, why are there different churches?

Then I looked again at Christ. I could not reject his divinity. I could see that the New Testament witnesses did teach he was God, that this was not a later pagan development. And I could see that modern Judaism is not the same as the Judaism at the time of our Lord: It is a later development and has split into sects which, to this day, remain in a constant state of flux and doctrinal disputation.

I continued to cling to my belief in Bible-only Christianity. The lifestyle and community of Evangelicalism is comforting, and my attendance at Catholic services seemed cold in comparison. But all this time I was growing increasingly disillusioned with anti-Catholic apologetics. Books like Loraine Boettner's *Roman Catholicism* (the classic anti-Catholic text) were in reality gross distortions of doctrine and history. I remember reading a book by one Evangelical who ridiculed the Catholic doctrine of sacramental intention. In fact he was ridiculing a misrepresentation. Classic Evangelical interpretation of the crucial Petrine texts, such as Matthew 16, was, I found, based on defective understanding. The play on the word "*petros*" was peripheral, as our Lord spoke Aramaic.

The overwhelming majority of modern-day Evangelical scholars now accept that Peter is the rock and that he was in a special way the recipient of the keys of authority. Just as the ancient kings of Israel delegated their keys of authority to a chief minister, Jesus had appointed Peter as his representative or vicar. Keys in any civilized culture represent power. I found that the anti-Catholic warping of the Church Fathers on this passage was quite deliberate. A theory is put forward that the Fathers are in disagreement that Peter is the rock. Careful examination of their writings reveals that they are not so much disagreeing as they are addressing different aspects of the text.

Contrary to Evangelical myth, there was abundant historical evidence for Peter's stay in Rome and for his establishment of its bishopric. Just as our Lord told Peter that flesh and blood had not revealed to him his divinity, I believe it was the gift of God that I could see in the Petrine texts the papacy in embryo. I was amazed to find that as early as the first century (when the Apostle John was still alive) the Bishop of Rome wrote to the Corinthian church to give instructions and to warn that ignoring this advice would involve them in grave danger.

As the centuries progressed the evidence for the papacy increased, and I found that there were sound answers to Evangelical objections. I remember being struck once by reading the comments of a Catholic in the visitor's book in the vestibule of an Anglican church: "Where Peter is, there is the Church." Those were the words of Ambrose in the fourth century, and they stuck in my mind. They had such an effect on me that I never fail to enter the same comment when signing the visitor's book of an Anglican church or cathedral. The Anglican church may have possession of the pre-Reformation church buildings, but it has not kept the ancient faith.

Despite a Catholic veneer painted over its surface in the nineteenth century, Anglicanism is Protestant. This has been manifested in women's ordination and other aberrations. Quite a few Evangelicals and educated Fundamentalists have sought refuge within Anglicanism. There they feel they have found liturgy and many aspects of Catholic ritual without needing to accept the sting of becoming a "Romanist."

It was the inherent confusion within Anglicanism that led me to examine the claims of the Catholic Church. While there were many things within Anglicanism that I loved, such as the fine tradition of choral music and my family associations, I realized that I must not be like the rich young man who placed his wealth before total commitment to Christ. If a person remains within Anglicanism because of sentimentality about a building or a taste for outward forms, he is in effect repeating the mistake of the rich young man. It is in reality a form of idolatry. The language of Cranmer may be beautiful, but it contains within it theological error that is destructive to the Catholic faith.

Many of Anglicanism's most beloved institutions are in fact appropriations of Catholic ritual and teaching. Far from finding that Anglo-Catholicism is the authentic Anglican tradition, I discovered that it is a comparatively recent development within Anglicanism. There is no real continuity with the seventeenth century high church divines, who were still firmly Protestant. Until the nineteenth century, no Anglicans prayed for the dead, or pleaded the interces-sion of the saints. The service of Holy Communion was rarely celebrated, the officiating minister did not wear the Catholic Eucharistic vestments, and there was strictly no reservation of the sacrament.

Indeed the Evangelical Anglicanism I knew was still true to the Reformation principles. I can remember the leftover consecrated communion elements of bread and wine being thrown away after the service. Indeed, Cardinal Newman had partly based his own denial of his Anglican orders on the fact that he could not believe that our Lord would leave himself to the care of the Anglican clergy, having witnessed the way many of its ranks viewed the Eucharist and treated the elements.

I next considered the Eastern Orthodox claim that it was the Church of Christ. But the role of Peter had become so clear to me that I could not accept their claims. Within the Eastern Orthodox communion I found beautiful liturgy, but a lack of magisterial clarity. For instance, until the 1930s every Christian church rejected artificial contraception as something intrinsically immoral. In 1930 the Anglican Church approved it, and since then many other churches, including the Orthodox, have followed suit.

Only the Catholic Church had stood firm on moral issues, even to the extent of losing the English nation in the sixteenth century because it would not compromise over a royal divorce. The Orthodox had deserted the successor of Peter for the imperial power of Constantinople and later that of St. Petersburg. They had put their trust in princes, and in the end this trust had failed them.

While this seemed to show me that the rock of the Catholic Church was firm, I was disturbed by the grass-roots liberalism of some of the Catholic people. Then I realized that in the parable of the house built on the rock, the house is battered by rain and wind. And I took the lesson that eccentrics and dissenters would not demolish the house. They might pound away at the rock, but they could never destroy it.

I found that as with our Lord, the main opposition was in three key areas. At the time of his earthly ministry, the religious authorities were appalled by his claim to be God, his claim to forgive sins, and his assertion that to have eternal life one must eat and drink his body and blood. The same opposition is virulently continued by Evangelicals today. Well, do I remember how, as an Evangelical, I despised the Catholic teaching of confession to a priest, the belief in transubstantiation, the Mass, and the infallibility of the pope and the Church. "Only God can be infallible," I would declare.

Close examination also showed that the Catholic doctrine on Mary was rooted in the Word of God and was not a pagan import. The fact that pagan religions have goddesses does not invalidate the Catholic teaching on Mary. Does the pagan belief in sacrifices and temples invalidate biblical concepts of sacrifice and temple? I found that Catholics do not regard Mary as divine and do not worship her. Lighting a candle in front of her statue is no more idolatrous than laying a wreath before the statute of Oliver Cromwell, as the members of the Protestant Truth Society ceremoniously do.

The Catholic doctrine of the communion of saints became real to me. If "the prayer of a righteous man avails much," the dead in the Lord, who are the spirits of just men made perfect, would make superlative intercession for us. This is wonderfully illustrated by the twenty-four elders representing the Old and New Testament saints who offer up prayer to God (Rev. 5:8).

Before I made my entry into the Catholic Church, a final line of appeal from concerned Evangelicals was that the personal lives of Catholics are in many cases disastrous. This was answered by my reading of Ronald Knox. He was brought up in a strongly Evangelical home and later converted to Catholicism. He once made the observation that if he left his umbrella at the back of a Methodist chapel, it would be there on his return, but probably not there if he had left it in a Catholic church. This was used by Methodists against Knox, but in reality it was a witness against them. Christ came to save sinners, and the net of the Church encompasses all men and women. It is not a club for middle-class Bible readers. Oscar Wilde summed it up brilliantly when he said, "The Church of England is for respectable people and the Catholic Church is for sinners."

The Church of Jesus Christ is a mixed lot, and the capital mistake of the Reformers was to believe that the Church must be composed 100 percent of the elect. Our Lord says, "Many are called, but few are chosen." While I have met some pretty dreadful Catholics, there are still many good people trying to lead holy lives according to the teachings of the Church. The unfortunate fact that Catholics disobey the teachings of the Church only confirms our Lord's warning that much will be required from those to whom much has been given. Judgment will begin with the household of God, and Catholics will be more culpable, as having had access to the truth. At the end of time God will separate the wheat and the tares.

I found Evangelicalism, like the Pharisees, concerned with superficial externals. I hope that does not sound harsh, but in effect many Bible Christians have built up a system of rules that condemn perfectly innocuous behavior as unchristian. Some view drinking as a sin and are convinced that our Lord drank only grape juice and that the miracle wine at Cana was strictly non-alcoholic. To some dancing is an abomination, to others smoking is the mark of a non-believer (although the nineteenth-century Baptist evangelist Spurgeon smoked). Others would not buy a lottery ticket—and yet would invest their money on the stock exchange. While it is impossible to stereotype Evangelical Christians, it is a fact that almost all are believers in contraception. God has charge of their money in tithing, but not charge of their bodies. I found Bible-only Christianity to be a set of subjective beliefs.

I am not alone. In recent years many conservative Evangelicals have entered the Catholic faith. They have done so even though the road to the Catholic Church was blocked by misrepresentations and opposition. Surely this is because of the grace of God, as there always exists opposition to the Catholic Church, opposition which is a fulfillment of our Lord's words. The opposition comes from secularism, materialism, modernism, and other philosophies, all of which reject the unique claims of the Catholic Church.

The Church is that small stone, envisioned by Daniel, that shatters the false image. It is the mustard seed that grows into a mighty bush. It is the way foretold by Isaiah in which foolish men would not err. It is the house founded on the rock. In the wise words of a Catholic prelate, Herbert Cardinal Vaughn (1832–1903):

> It is a common practice with the opponents of the Catholic Church to endeavor to hold souls back by arraigning before them a multitude of difficulties and objections against the doctrines of the Church. To this two things may be said. First, it would be easy to string together a most formidable array of difficulties quoted and examined by Catholic theologians in their great scientific works on theology. But it is obvious that it would be necessary to be a trained theologian, or to spend a lifetime in research, were it needful to give detailed answers to them all. Then there are works, like those of

anti-Catholic writers, written in order to blind and mislead: made up of calumnies, misquotations, and a calculated admixture of truth and error. These are often intended to shock and alienate the moral sense quite as much as the intellectual. If they do not finally succeed in this, at least they may succeed in creating perplexity, anxiety, and delay. Now, instead of entering into a maze of objections, into a labyrinth of difficulties, a shorter and more satisfactory course should be taken. First find the divine teacher, find the supreme shepherd, find the Vicar of Christ. Concentrate all your mental and moral faculties upon the head of God's Church upon earth. This is the key to the situation.

# 10

# Heaven Scent

## *Craig Turner*

It is in search of strays like me that Christ said he would leave the other ninety-nine. But in my case, I prefer to think, he chose to send his very own mother.

I was born and raised Presbyterian. While growing up I attended a Presbyterian church in Houston, a large, hip congregation that boasted the Joyful Noise Choir and listened to fiery sermons peppered with love and forgiveness. I entered college fully immersed in my faith, but the lack of spiritual and moral accountability over the next few years, coupled with the secular character of the curriculum and teaching, sent me into a downward spiral that ended in agnosticism. Following graduation I dabbled in Taoism and Buddhism. Finally, after an abortive attempt to join the Buddhist Temple in downtown Washington, D.C. (the Asian proprietors couldn't understand my intentions), I began a concerted effort to find meaning and truth.

I studied Nietzsche, Sartre, Plato, and other great thinkers. I spent weekends reading volumes of philosophy and attended courses in metaphysics and phenomenology. By my late twenties, my spiral had taken me to the bottom, and I became entrenched in atheism, believing that the almighty intellect could provide all there is to know about the universe.

It was the summer of 1991. I was living in an old decrepit mansion lying in the shadows of Washington's monuments and leading a routine life as the director of communications for an association of government contractors. One day a coworker, Beth, and her husband, Steve, returned from a trip to the site of alleged Marian apparitions. They told tales of smelling invisible roses in mysterious places, of rosary beads turning to gold, and of a miracle in the sun. Baffled and a little miffed, I said that these were interesting experiences but they did not prove any kind of transcendent Spirit.

Little did I know that these friends had taken with them a petition to the Virgin Mary, written on plain white paper, requesting my conversion. Had I known, I would have laughed and told them not to get their hopes up. The universe, as I well knew, was governed by the laws of physics, not by spirits and demons, and submitting petitions to people long dead would have sounded to me like hocus-pocus.

But these persistent friends, who had recently returned to the Catholic Church after staying away for years, took it upon themselves to evangelize me. They gave me a book to read, *Life in Christ*. Their plan was to reach me through logic and theology. I read two pages and returned the book. Life went on, and I didn't dwell on their experiences or their convictions.

Then in May of 1992 a strange thing happened to me. I began to sense strongly a mysterious message: "Pray, pray, pray!" Over and over, I felt this urgent calling and, though inaudible, it was almost as clear to me as if someone were speaking the words. As an atheist I did not take kindly to cryptic messages and mysterious feelings. I tried to ignore it, much as I would a cold or the flu, knowing that these things simply go away. But the message continued, day after day, for two weeks. It was as if a neon sign were blinking in the fog and I was able to make out a single word: "Pray!"

Finally, I decided to acquiesce. Maybe that would make the message go away. One night I got ready for sleep, went into my room, and lay face down on my bed. After a few minutes, I lifted my head up, put my hands together, and talked a little to God. I had not prayed in so long that I was not sure what to say. Like any conversation with a friend one hasn't seen in a long time, it was awkward at first. After about four minutes I said, "Well, I guess that's it," and I went to sleep.

After that I started praying daily. As my prayer life developed, I began to realize that I was not leading the life I should. The most immediate and urgent change was a call to chastity. My girlfriend,

Kathleen, and I discussed it at length and reached an agreement. We chose a date when we would begin living chastely. This date came—and then it went. We chose another date, realizing it would take greater effort to succeed, but this too came and went without success. Finally, we chose a third date. We realized it was imperative that we succeed. We set down rules to live by, reminded each other of the importance of the endeavor, and agreed to give as much effort as we were capable of. The date we chose to start this new life was Labor Day 1992—the day we were struck by lightning.

Labor Day was approaching and Kathleen and I had decided to spend the holiday camping in a remote region of Ontario, Canada, called Algonquin Park. We bought new camping gear and a new tent and got plane tickets to Toronto. Arriving in Toronto, we spent the night there, rented a car, and started the long trip north to the park. We rented canoes at one of the tiny settlements inside the park, put our gear in, and started paddling south.

We camped beside Ragged Lake, a beautiful lake that stretches its crooked fingers in many directions through the small mountains. For two days we made mapless paddles and treks throughout the area, investigating the territory but not getting too far away from our campsite because we found that we had accidentally left our map of the park back in the car. These were possibly the most beautiful days we had ever seen.

The morning of the third day—Labor Day—we awoke in our tent to the sound of distant thunder. A storm was coming and I intended to sleep through it, but Kathleen suggested that we cover up our gear to keep it dry. Getting up, I stowed our belongings beneath the overturned canoes and then crawled back into my sleeping bag on the right side of the tent. The rain had already begun to fall, and the storm was soon upon us. Light rain quickly became heavy, then came high winds, and finally lightning cracking and booming above. After a particularly loud zap that sounded like a cannon blast, Kathleen asked me, "Are we going to get struck by lightning?"

I laughed and responded with assurance, "No. There are too

many tall trees around." Everyone knows that lightning will strike the tallest object first, and camping inside a forest would guarantee that we wouldn't be hit.

Less than a minute later, as I was lying on my left side facing Kathleen, the most incredible pain hit me from all sides at once and surged throughout my body. I found myself screaming uncontrollably. The pain was so excruciating that at that instant I was sure this was the moment of my death. Every inch of my body was under intense and agonizing torture. Then, after what was probably two or three seconds, the pain departed and the world around me went black.

After a moment of unconsciousness, I awoke, completely paralyzed and as dazed as if I were coming out of a coma. Kathleen was lying on her back moaning in pain. "My legs. My legs. I can't feel my legs."

I couldn't feel anything in my body, but I wanted to move my arm to cover her in case something should fall on us from above. "Come closer," I moaned. It took every ounce of energy in my body to lift my right arm and place it on top of her. For several terrifying minutes after this we were unable to move at all. Then, slowly, we were able to sit up. Kathleen's legs were paralyzed and numb for another few minutes.

After about ten minutes more, we were somewhat coherent and able to move a little more. My left knee and shoulder throbbed. It felt like someone had hit them with an axe. We smelled smoke. This turned out to be the burned back of Kathleen's sweatshirt and the singed hairs on my arms. Later we would find some gray hairs on my head.

After a couple of hours, we packed up and canoed through the intermittent drizzle to a ranger station. We discovered as we left our campsite that the bolt of lightning had somehow threaded its way among the tall trees and had blasted a small tree near our tent. It blew apart the poor little tree, and the charge went through the root system and up into us—our tent was perched on top of the roots. My left shoulder had been directly on top of the main root, and the lightning had passed through my body and jumped from my left knee into Kathleen's legs. From there it moved down to Kathleen's ankle and back into the ground. This lightning, we think, was the kind that seems to flicker on and off a few times before going out, thus accounting for the length of the shock itself.

We later got checked at a hospital (the doctor didn't believe our story—he only took my blood pressure and barely even talked to Kathleen) and then retreated in disgrace back to Toronto. For about a day and a half after the incident, Kathleen and I both suffered from strange variations in hunger, from being famished one moment to satisfied the next. For a week I suffered blurred vision, migraine headaches, depression, and memory loss.

The next day we flew back to Washington, D.C. Kathleen was still shaken up by the whole event and, as a Catholic, had decided that she should talk to a priest. After several phone calls, she managed to get in touch with a priest who was willing to meet her that evening.

"Do you want to go?" she asked me.

"Sure, I'll drive you," I said. "I've never met a priest."

After a short wait in the St. Agnes Church rectory, Fr. Donahue came slowly down the stairs. He walked with two canes because of a spinal injury—he had been shot by a sniper when he was a teenager. He turned out to be one of the most supremely nice human beings I have ever met.

After Kathleen had talked to Fr. Donahue in his office for about a half hour, she stuck her smiling face out the door and invited me in. We spent another ten minutes or so talking to him together about our experience in Canada, and then, just as we were about to leave, he said to us, "Before you go, I want to give you something." He made his way with his canes over to the closet and returned with two small platinum objects.

"These," he said, "are Miraculous Medals. I want to give one to each of you before you go."

He gave us a brochure telling the fascinating story behind the Miraculous Medal: St. Catherine Labouré was awakened by an angel in the middle of the night and led down corridors of flickering candles in her convent. When they arrived at the chapel, she was instructed to wait. After kneeling in a pew for a short time, she heard the rustle of silk. Mary appeared to her in splendor and with great kindness explained the reason for her visit. She then showed Catherine the vision of a medal with an image of Mary surrounded by the words: "O Mary, conceived without sin, pray for us who have recourse to thee."

"Have a medal struck in this image," Mary said to her. "All who wear it will receive great graces."

The medal was originally called the Medal of the Immaculate Conception, but so many unusual and inexplicable events were associated with those who wore it that it soon became known as the Miraculous Medal.

"Great," I said. "I used to have a shark's tooth but I lost it. I can wear this instead."

Fr. Donahue blessed the medals and put them around our necks, and we went on our way.

About a week after receiving the Miraculous Medal, something tremendous began to happen. I began to "hear" the prayers of my Catholic friends Beth and Steve. It was not with words, but audible through inspiration, like a solid tug on an invisible rope. As it continued each day—I could not discern what the message was nor could I fathom why they were doing it—I became convinced beyond doubt that they were praying for me. I mentioned it to Kathleen.

"I suppose you could be sensing their prayers," she responded.

A week later the sensation had grown to be so strong that I said, "Kathleen, I know that Steve and Beth are praying for me. They have never indicated to me in any way that they were praying for me, but I'm sure it's true."

"I'm sure it could be true," she said. "Why don't you ask them?"

About a week later, Steve and Beth and I were shopping. As we walked back to our cars I knew there would be no better time to ask perhaps the silliest question I had ever dreamed up. As we stood there talking, I said, "Steve, I have a question for you. Have . . . have you . . . have you been praying for me?" I stammered out the question and sort of ducked in fear of his laughter.

Steve looked at me and said matter-of-factly, "I sure have."

"I knew it! Somehow I knew it!" I cried. "I felt it. I knew you were praying for me. I even told Kathleen. I told her twice, and I even said that I knew you guys were praying for me. You have to believe me. I really did know somehow."

"I do believe you."

"No, really. I could feel you praying for me!"

During the next ten minutes, Steve and Beth recounted the great extent to which they had committed themselves to praying for me. They told me that they were saying prayers almost daily for my conversion, and that in the beginning I was so far away from believing in God that they thought I was a hopeless case. They had asked St. Jude for help.

Then Beth said to me, "Craig, do you know what prayer we were saying for you?"

"No. What?"

"The Miraculous Medal novena."

"What!" I cried out. "You prayed the prayer of the Miraculous Medal?" I yanked the chain with the Miraculous Medal out from underneath my shirt. "Do you realize that I was given this medal only a couple of weeks ago by a priest? This is too much! Before that I had never even heard of one before."

We spent the next few minutes talking about the Miraculous Medal and the prayer, and about the sense I had had that Steve and Beth were praying for me. I left that night perplexed but happy.

The next morning I sat at my desk drinking coffee and thinking about what had happened the night before. I had always known that my vision of the universe was not the only one. It couldn't be. It is like looking through the end of a telescope, thinking that what we see constitutes the infinitude of reality. What was happening to me, I thought, was an expansion of my field of vision through my telescope, so that I was able to see more of reality than I could previously, albeit not the entirety. I knew beyond any doubt, though, that I had heard my friends' prayers. This was astounding.

If something was really going on, something I couldn't explain that was spiritual or religious, I couldn't simply sit around waiting for things to happen to me. I had to do something in return.

I thought hard about what to do. A link was connecting all these events—Beth and Steve's pilgrimage, my receiving the Miraculous Medal, my friends praying the Miraculous Medal novena for me, and my sensing their prayers—and that link was the Blessed Mother. I decided my one step forward should be to learn the Hail Mary.

I obtained a brochure that explained how to pray the rosary. I had to meet Steve at their apartment in Alexandria, Virginia, and it would be the opportune time as I drove to learn the prayer. I left work and headed south on the Beltway. Holding the brochure with my right hand and steering with my left, I maneuvered the crowded highway repeating the words of the prayer for half an hour until I reached Alexandria.

As I prayed I thought about what the words meant. The first half of the prayer is a salutation, an invocation of praise meant to honor Mary and her role in Christianity. The second half of the prayer is a request to Mary that she intercede on our behalf and bestow upon us the graces that she administers.

When I reached Alexandria I had time to kill before Steve got home from work. The only parking place I could find was in front of the Alexandria Coffee Company. I bought Kathleen a pound of coffee, tossed it onto the passenger seat of my car, and drove to Steve's apartment.

When I arrived, Steve had just come home. Beth was at the gym and he was making himself dinner. As I sat down at the kitchen table, he microwaved a chicken sandwich and sat down to talk with me. His dinner smelled strongly of processed food, and I kidded him about it. As we sat at the table discussing football and other topics, I caught the faint smell of something different. I thought nothing of it, of course, until the same smell drifted by, only stronger. Suddenly, the most powerful scent of roses I had ever encountered came over me. The smell was so powerful it nearly knocked my head back.

"Steve, where are the roses?" I asked. From the smell it was clear that there had to be least a few dozen fresh roses nearby.

"What roses?" Steve said.

I laughed and swiveled around in my chair to look at his apartment. "The roses. Where are the roses?"

The scent washed over me, getting stronger and stronger, like waves hitting a beach. The waves increased until the overwhelming smell of roses surrounded me.

"We don't have any roses here," Steve said, giving me a curious look.

"Beth must wear rose perfume," I said.

Steve thought for a moment. "No. Beth doesn't have any rose perfume."

I got up and walked around the apartment. It was as if I were in a room piled high with roses, their fragrance everywhere, but I couldn't find any.

"You mean you don't smell any roses?" I asked.

"No, I don't."

As I walked around the apartment sniffing the air and looking in vain for roses that didn't exist, Steve said to me, "Craig! You're being visited by the Blessed Mother!"

I immediately remembered Steve and Beth's episode with roses during their pilgrimage, a story I had heard more than a year before and had forgotten, and I knew what Steve meant. But this was so far from any sort of reality that I would even consider that I wheeled around and said, "That's bull, man." I stormed around the living room, then the dining area, then the kitchen, then the study, looking for roses I knew had to be there.

I returned to my chair and sat down. "Come here," I said to Steve. I lifted my hand up next to my face where I wanted him to be. "Put your face right here."

Steve moved closer to me and leaned forward so his head was right next to mine.

"Now take a deep breath." He breathed in deeply and held it. "You don't smell roses? And don't lie!"

He laughed and moved back to his side of the kitchen table, smiling as if he understood my dilemma. "I don't smell any roses," he said again.

Just then Beth returned home from the gym. She walked in, turned around, and no doubt saw two men sitting at the kitchen table with looks of awe on their faces. She stopped in her tracks and said, "What happened?"

"Craig is smelling roses," Steve said.

"What!" Quickly Beth shut the door. She threw her bags onto the floor and sat down in the chair next to me. "Craig!" she exclaimed.

"Beth," I said, looking at her sternly. "I want you to take a deep breath and tell me what you smell."

Beth drew a long, deep breath, exhaled, and looked at me seriously. She shook her head. "Nothing."

After I had calmed down a bit, Beth, recalling her own experience, asked, "It smells perfumey, right?"

"Yes!" I said.

A few minutes later she said, "And it comes in waves. . . ."

"Yes!" I exclaimed again. It *did* come in waves. Unless she had had the same experience, how could she have made that comment?

I spent fifty minutes in their apartment that day. The first twenty minutes I smelled nothing but stale apartment air and the smell of a microwaved chicken sandwich. Then the overpowering aroma of roses stayed in the air for the next thirty minutes until I left.

When I climbed into my car, I was ecstatic. I sniffed the air inside my car, but all I smelled was the very strong odor of coffee from the bag of beans I had bought an hour earlier. I fired up the engine and drove away giddy with joy. How in the world could something like this happen?

I was so happy, in fact, that I decided to pray the Hail Mary again. I began with the words, "Hail Mary . . ." but before I could even finish the short prayer the strong odor of coffee was suddenly overwhelmed by the smell of roses. Right there, sitting in my car—the very same car that I drove to work every day of the week and had owned for more than three years—it was as if roses were piled up to my neck. During the entire drive home, I smelled roses and not just roses, but overwhelming and intense

ROSES.

Sitting in Fr. Donahue's office, I explained to him that I had returned because I had had some experiences that were inexplicable to me and wondered if he could shed some light on them. I related my friends' experiences staring into the sun, their encounter with the rose scent, my undeniable conviction—confirmed by them—that they were praying for me, and then my smelling roses in their apartment after having prayed the Hail Mary for the first time. What in heck was going on here?

"Well, Craig, experiences such as smelling roses do happen. There are stories throughout history in which Christians were converted by means of dramatic events. But let me give you some words of caution: These experiences happen, if at all, only a few times during a person's life. These little gifts, called graces, are used to call people closer to God. Don't expect them to happen forever. If we were to get these signs all the time, we would not be required to believe with faith. We also might believe and act as we are supposed to only in order to continue to get these signs. In other words, God doesn't want us to act in a way that is pleasing to him just so we can get the prize from time to time. Just like you don't want to give candy to a child too often—if you do, the child is simply doing what you want in order to get more candy."

As an atheist—or, more accurately, as a former atheist—I could no longer presume that God didn't have a hand in these events. It was time to act, time for me to do something instead of merely waiting for things to happen to me.

After work one day I drove to one of the most majestic and beautiful buildings that I have ever visited: the Basilica of the National Shrine of the Immaculate Conception. I had come to pray my first rosary. It was, I suppose, a way of saying thank you. Inside was the beautiful, smoky fragrance Catholic churches often retain from the incense that burns as a symbol of our prayers rising toward heaven. I walked through the nave of the church admiring the crimson and blue stained glass on either side until I found what I was looking for: a small shrine, like a grotto built into the side of the church, with candles burning on either side and a small altar at the front. Above the altar was an enormous replica of the medal I wore around my neck. This was the Shrine of the Miraculous Medal.

I entered the little shrine and knelt in a pew. After a few moments I began to pray. I gave thanks for having been given the grace to smell roses and for having been led on a path—by now it was undeniable—toward prayer and the Church. There was nothing I could say or do that could repay what had been given to me. I was truly and deeply grateful.

After this prayer I pulled out the brochure I carried on me which explained how to say the rosary, took out my rosary beads, and started from the beginning. The first few prayers of the rosary were tricky. The middle section was easy to learn and was an enchanting way to meditate on the life of Christ. Then, as I prayed the final "Hail, Holy Queen," I felt a beautiful, inexplicable peace come over me. It was a realization that somehow, despite all the evil and chaos in the world, harmony really does exist, and love is the true, permanent foundation of our existence.

As I said the final words, "Pray for us, O holy Mother of God, that we may be made worthy of the promises of Christ," a familiar smell came to me. It was as if ten crates of roses had been dumped in front of me—no, a hundred crates of roses—a smell so strong it was almost intoxicating.

I knelt there in that beautiful little shrine, surrounded by white flickering candles, and breathed in the fragrance of eternity.

[Craig Turner was confirmed into the Catholic Church at the Easter Vigil Mass of 1993. Five months later, he and Kathleen were married and became one in Christ and in his Church. Craig immersed himself in the study of the faith, became a CCD teacher, lector, and Eucharistic minister, and has shared his story in person with many groups. He also has been involved in the pro-life movement through the National Committee for Human Life Amendment, funded by the U.S. Catholic Bishops. Craig and Kathleen and their son, Nicholas, live in Burke, Virginia.—ed.]

## 11

# From Promise to Fulfillment

## *Rosalind Moss*

### Christmas 1978

"Ros, I'm going to midnight Mass—you're welcome to come."

I'm welcome to come? To a Catholic church? For Mass? Oy! What's a Jewish Evangelical to do?

There was only one thing I could do: I would accompany my brother. But I would be risking the effects of venturing into the heart of "Satan's system." Still, it would be a risk worth taking if, through it, I could persuade David of the error and the danger of that Church and rescue him from the unthinkable fate of becoming Catholic.

Off we went. It was a cold but beautiful and still Christmas Eve in upstate New York. Snowflakes dropped like lace petals. As we approached the small church, I had to fight the sense of beauty and warmth that shone from the stained glass windows. I wasn't about to let myself be taken in by what I knew was false. It would be just like Satan to make error so enticing.

As we climbed the front steps and entered the church, I think I held my breath. People coming in around us dipped their fingers in a small basin of water and crossed themselves. Paganism, I thought. What has *that* to do with knowing Christ as your personal Lord and Savior? Most of the people genuflected before entering a pew. Another pagan ritual, I supposed. How could my brother be drawn to this? What was his problem? What was missing from his Evangelical faith? How could he have found the truth of Christianity, that Jesus Christ is indeed the Jewish Messiah, God come to earth, and still be looking further—looking into the Catholic Church of all places?

My thoughts went back to our childhood, to our Jewish home in Brooklyn. I was the middle child of three. My brother David was two years older and my sister Susan was not quite three years younger. From my earliest years I can recall being filled with a sense of grace (though I wouldn't have known that word for it). We had been taught there were basically two kinds of people in the world: Jews and non-Jews. And since the Jews were God's chosen people, I felt it a great gift to have been born of Jewish seed. Certainly, I thought then, it was not a matter for pride; I had nothing to do with my birth. In fact, I remember, in my child's mind, asking myself . . . "If we have the *true* God, who does the rest of the world have?" Certainly those who were not of the Hebrew race had no choice in their birth either, so surely they could not be blamed for not knowing the God of Abraham. Such a mystery I was content to leave with God, who knew what I did not.

I loved our traditions. Challah baking in the oven, the celebration of Chanukah (to commemorate the victory of Judah Maccabee against Antiochus Epiphanes, King of Syria, and the miracle of the oil that burned for eight days in the temple), Purim (the celebration of Esther's victory over the evil Haman in his attempt to destroy the Jewish people), Sukkot (a taste of what it might have been like to live in booths in the wilderness during God's protection of the Israelites through their forty years of wandering), Shavuot (rejoicing over the giving of the Law at Mt. Sinai), and Rosh Hashanah, the Jewish New Year (brought in by the blowing of a ram's horn). I recall one Rosh Hashanah when the entire neighborhood joined in the celebration, whether they wished to or not, as David blew the ram's horn outside our apartment building in Brooklyn. Ten days later came Yom Kippur, the Day of Atonement, the holiest day of all, which we spent fasting and praying in *schul* (Yiddish for "synagogue"), asking God to forgive our sins.

As the world celebrated Easter, we sat down to the Passover table, which, in the religious calendar, begins the feast year. We were not Orthodox Jews, and so our observance was only a partial rendering of what might have been. Yet we would make sure that every bit of leaven was out of the house for the eight days of Passover.

We loved Pesach (Passover). We loved the food we got to eat at that time each year: matzah with chicken fat, matzah brei, special noodle kugel, gefilte fish, and horseradish on everything! And we loved the Seder (Passover service). If our extended family gathered at only one time of year, it was at Passover. Days of preparation climaxed around a long table filled with elements that told the story of our people's deliverance from slavery in Egypt (matzah, parsley, salt water, bitter herbs, charoset, a roasted lamb shank). My Uncle Murray would lead us through the Passover Haggadah, recounting the journey, in word and song, partaking of the symbolic foods along the way, singing the Hallel (Psalms 113-118), and drinking of the four cups of wine.

Two of the rituals became embedded in my memory. One was the first of four questions which began the Seder: "Why is this night different from all others?" As we sang of Moses leading the Israelites to freedom through the sea, I knew that we, thousands of years later, were a part of that story and that our freedom as a people came from that deliverance. This night indeed was different from all others and served as a reminder of, and in a sense a participation in, that drama of deliverance, and gave us the opportunity to thank God, who did not and would not abandon his people.

The second ritual that I would recall long after our family traditions had ceased was the Seder's end. Regardless of what had transpired during the evening—or during the year, for that matter—we would leave the Passover table singing, "Next year in Jerusalem." One year, maybe next year, the Messiah would come, and when he did, we would be gathered as a people from the four corners of the earth to Jerusalem to be with him in his kingdom, the kingdom he would establish on earth. There would be peace then, and all things would be made new.

I remember the year it was my turn to see if the Messiah had come and if (perhaps!) he were waiting outside our house at the door left ajar for him at every Passover. My legs were shaking as I set off. And I was filled with disappointment and relief (I'm not sure in what proportion) to find the hallway empty of the long-awaited Guest.

"Next year in Jerusalem," we'd sing as we left the table. Next year, when he comes.

*"Thou hast made us for thyself, O Lord . . ."*

If only I had known those blessed words of Augustine through the years of emptiness that followed. What was missing from my Jewish upbringing? Many things, perhaps, but nothing that could answer the silent questions I lived with from the time I was a young child: "Why are we here? Why do we exist? What will our life on earth have been for?"

My brother David searched for truth. For years he searched. "What makes you think there's such a thing as truth?" I thought. "And what makes you think you can find it? Suppose truth meant that God really existed. Then what? How would knowing that change your life?"

I never searched. I am because of what is, I figured. If "what is" means there's a God, therefore I am. If "what is" means there's *no* God, therefore I am. My knowledge or lack of it doesn't determine "what is," so why know? How can *knowing* make a difference in one's life?

David declared himself an atheist; I called myself an agnostic. You have to know a *lot*, I thought, to *know* there's no God. I jumped into business in New York City, had an active social life, and did my best to survive the consuming agony of my heart that there was no reason to exist. No amount of love, money, or success could dispel the sense of purposelessness I lived with.

*". . . and our hearts are restless until they find their rest in thee."*

An unexpected phone call from David in the summer of 1976 was about to change the course of my life. He phoned to tell me some news involving his wife of twelve years, Janet.

"Ros," he said, "Janet has come to believe in Christ. She's been going to the Baptist church near our house. I haven't come to any conclusions yet, but as long as Janet has a strong conviction, the children will follow her. If and when I come to answers, I'll deal with them then."

I hung up the phone in shock. How could my brother love his children and let them be raised to believe in a *man*? Prophet, teacher, whoever Christ was, we're Jews. And *if* there's a God, we have a direct connection. We don't need to go through anyone.

I visited them that summer. In one of our marathon conversations, David told me about an article he had read that said there was such a thing as Jewish people, in this day, who believe that Jesus Christ (a name forbidden to us) was, in fact, the Jewish Messiah we had been waiting for.

The Messiah? They believed the Messiah had come? Already? How could that be possible? If there were a Messiah, if the faith of my childhood were true, he was the only hope the world had. He was to set up his kingdom. How could the Messiah have come and no one have a clue? He didn't make an impact when he came? There's no kingdom? No peace? Nothing? And he left? What an insanity that would be. How could we even consider such a thing? Obviously, those Jews who believed this were troubled, and their beliefs had nothing to do with me or with truth.

Not long after that conversation, I moved to California, and within three months my path crossed that of these so-called Jewish believers. They were handing out tracts in Westwood Village near UCLA. The tract read, "If being born hasn't given you much satisfaction, try being born again." Oh, if ever a message penetrated my heart! But I dared not let it show, not with these people. Not only did they affirm their belief that Christ was the Messiah, but they believed that he was God come to earth. God, a man?! The least educated Jew knew that a man can't be God, that one cannot even look on God and live.

But, what if? What if there's really a God and you could know that? Could knowing make a difference in your life? And what if, as they claimed, you could know him? A bit of *Twilight Zone* for me. I wasn't interested in what people concocted to help them deal with the emptiness of life. I'd rather live in despair all my life than live a lie. But if by chance they were onto something, I had nothing to lose by checking it out.

For months they tried to get the message through to me that Christ died for our sins, and that faith in him was the only way to know you would spend eternity with God. They might as well have spoken a foreign language—until one night, one life-changing night.

Twelve of them—Jewish believers (Jewish Evangelical Christians, I would later discover)—and I, at dinner, were deep in conversation about this supposed salvation drama. "For the sake of discussion," I interrupted, "let's say Christ died for your sins, my sins, and the sins of the world. Whatever that language means, let's say it happened. My question is, 'What for? Why did he do it? What was in his *mind* when he did that?'"

For the next two hours, those dear Christians took me through the sacrificial system of the Old Testament Scriptures (Tanach), which I had never known through all my years in synagogue. They explained that God *is*, that he is holy, and that he cannot come into the presence of sin. More, that the wages of sin is death, separation from God, now and through all eternity. They demonstrated through the Torah that God required the blood of a perfect offering to atone for the sins of man, and that as an individual would bring that offering (a bull, goat, or lamb) to the altar, he would place his hand on the head of that animal. It was symbolic of the sins being transferred from the individual onto the offering. And that lamb, through no fault of its own, who now bore the sins of the individual would then be slain and its blood shed on the altar as an offering to God, in payment of that person's sin.

"Why?" I thought. Why would God put an innocent animal to death for my sin? Put me to death. It made no sense to me, but it began to get through to me that sin was no light issue to God. They explained further that the blood of tens of thousands of lambs slain through 1,500 years of that sacrificial system could not take away sin, nor had these sacrifices the power to change the heart of the worshipper. Those sacrifices were a sign, rather, a sign that pointed to the one who would one day come and take upon himself—not the sin of a person for a time, but the sin of all men—past, present, and future—for all time.

I thought I had fairly well grasped their explanation to this point, but could never have anticipated what followed. "When Jesus came," they said, "John the Baptist looked at him and said, '*Behold, the Lamb of God who takes away the sin of the world . . . .*'"

Time stopped. I don't recall another word they said. I sat at that restaurant table shattered. The Lamb? *The* Lamb? The Lamb to which every Old Testament lamb pointed, who died for the sins of the world . . . and mine? And the reason his blood alone could atone was because it was the blood of the sinless, spotless Son of God? But how can a man be God? He cannot. But that night I realized for the first time that, while a man cannot be God, God can become a man; he can do anything he wants to do. It wasn't for me to tell him how to be God!

It was not too long after that most blessed of nights that I gave my life to that incomparable Lamb who changed my life overnight and gave me, at last, a purpose for every second I breathe. The world was new and I a new creation in him. How I wished for a ladder to reach the moon and tell the world of such a Savior!

Some months later I told the head of the advertising company for which I worked that I was not going to continue on with them to open up a San Francisco branch office for which they had hired me. Certainly there was nothing wrong with Christians being in business, but God had changed my heart and I wasn't sure where I belonged anymore.

"Why do you have to be a fanatic?" he responded. "Why can't you have this thing in balance: eight hours of work, eight hours of sleep, and eight hours of God!"

"I can't," I tried in vain to explain. "Think of one born blind, who suddenly, one day, can see. He can't even appreciate a tree yet, because he's too overwhelmed with the fact that he even sees that tree!" Settle down? Eight hours a day?

I went to work for a halfway house for troubled teens, jumped into Bible study at my nondenominational Evangelical church, and worked in every form of neighborhood outreach, including jails and juvenile halls. I jettisoned every thing and every relationship that would not honor the God who loved me and gave himself for me.

A year later, my brother, who a year earlier had thought my socalled Christianity was not much more than an emotional experience, called from New York to tell me that he had given his life to Christ, believing him to be the Messiah indeed and God come to earth. Shortly after, my sister, who also had been searching, came to put her trust in Christ. What joy for the three of us to have come to believe. "Infinite, marvelous, matchless grace. . . ."

*". . . our hearts are restless until they find their rest in Thee."*

"Ros," David began, in what was to be one of many long phone conversations, "something's wrong. I believe the Bible is the word of God and as such, infallible. But how is it that so many men, pastors who love God, who study the Word of God in humility and sincerity and with all the tools of biblical interpretation, come out with such different understandings of Scripture, and in such crucial areas? If Christ established his Church on earth and left us his word, wouldn't he have left us a way to know what he *meant* by what he said?"

"Yes, David, but we see through a glass dimly. One day we'll know as we are known. For now, we simply do the best we can."

David didn't buy it. He said that Christ had prayed that we would be one as he and the Father are one. How could he have established his Church on earth and left us to the confusion of thousands of denominations with new ones budding almost daily?

Again David searched. Within a year, he was seriously looking into the Catholic Church. Oh no, I thought, *anything* but Catholic! If David only knew what I knew. My first Bible study was taught by an ex-Catholic who had been taught by an ex-priest, so I had gotten the truth of Catholicism from the horse's mouth: It was a cult, a false religious system leading millions astray. Surely David was not about to be taken in by such deception.

Before long, he was studying with a monk. That did it! I flew to

New York and met with David and the monk. For hours we went back and forth on Reformation issues. I thought for sure I was in the presence of one of Satan's emissaries.

Christmas Eve came a few days later and I agreed to accompany David to midnight Mass. It would be the first time I'd ever gone to a Catholic Mass.

## Christmas 1978 (to continue where the story began):

As Mass began and the procession of people and priest moved slowly down the central aisle toward the front altar, the foreign character of this cult began to have a faint sense of familiarity. As I took in the surroundings—the reverence, the posture in prayer, the formality of the liturgy, the sacredness with which the Word of God was handled and read, the candles, the *appearance* of worship (but how could this *truly* be worship? I was in a *Catholic church!*)— the sense of familiarity turned to a measure of horror.

The Mass ended. We filed out of the church with everyone else, past the water basins into which people again dipped their fingers, past the priest with whom I'd have no contact under any circumstances, down the steps and toward the car in silence.

"Whad'ya think?" David asked as we began the half-hour drive home. I couldn't even speak; I was in shock and sick inside, but could not put my finger on why. Not a word the entire trip home. When we reached the door, David begged, "Say *something*, anything." I realized what was bothering me so deeply. "David, *that* is a *synagogue*—but with Christ!"

"That's right!"

"No!" I said "That's wrong!" What was David's problem? Did he have a hang-up from our Jewish background—the liturgy, the aesthetics? Didn't he understand that Christ was the end to which it all pointed?

Two months later David was Catholic. I grieved. But all wasn't necessarily lost. There was still a ray of hope: perhaps as he plunged into the depths of that "system," he would see it for what it was. Surely, if he had *truly* given his life to Christ, he couldn't remain Catholic. But the passage of time only shattered my hope and deepened David's conviction that the Catholic Church was the Church Christ had established.

In the ten-year span that followed, I completed the Bible Institute program at my church, went through mission training, became part of the Bible Institute staff, and earned an M.A. in Ministry at Talbot Theological Seminary on the Biola University campus in La Mirada, California. During my time at Talbot, I worked full-time as chaplain of a women's jail facility in Lancaster, California.

It was the summer of 1990. I would transition from the jail chaplaincy to the staff of an Evangelical church as director of women's ministries. The pastor of this particular church within the "Friends" denomination was an ex-Catholic with Baptist training. He had reinstituted the ordinances of baptism and communion seventeenth century. With the month of June to myself, I spent two weeks with David and my sister, Susan, in New York. We barely came up for air the entire time as we wrestled with every issue of faith.

At a seemingly inopportune moment (not that there ever would have been an opportune one), David handed me a magazine:

"Have you ever seen this?"

"*This Rock*? No."

"It's a Catholic apologetics publication. You might be interested."

A Catholic *apologetics* magazine? What kind of a phenomenon was that? Catholics have a defense for their faith? I had never met a Catholic who knew his faith. No Catholic ever told me the gospel.

But there was something more. I never knew Catholics *cared* that anyone know it. I thought, "If you even *think* you have the truth, and the truth means your soul, and the souls of everyone alive on the face of the earth, how do you keep that to yourself?"

I had my first measure of respect for any group of Catholics who would want the world to know what they believe. I took the magazine back with me to California and in it came across a full-page advertisement:

*Presbyterian Minister Becomes Catholic*

His name was Scott Hahn. I had never heard of him. I had never heard of such a thing. I thought, I don't care what his title was, or what his function was, he could not have known Christ, he could not have had a personal relationship with the Lord Jesus Christ, and then have become Catholic. Perhaps he wasn't a Christian when he was a Presbyterian and became one when he entered the Catholic Church, not knowing better than to buy in to all that stuff. But because his background was close enough to mine, theologically, I ordered the set of four tapes offered in the ad.

A week from my starting date at the Friends church, while packing up my apartment in Lancaster, I listened to the tapes, which contained Scott Hahn's testimony and a two-part debate with a Presbyterian theologian on the Reformation issues of *sola scriptura* and *sola fide* (scripture alone and faith alone). Scott Hahn was the stronger of the two, I had to admit. But it wasn't because he had the truth, I thought, it was because he was the better able to articulate his position. I listened in growing frustration, thinking of all that the Presbyterian minister did not say but surely must know.

Toward the conclusion of the debate, each was given fifteen minutes to summarize his position. In Scott Hahn's concluding remarks, he said that if you look into the claims of the Catholic Church—two thousand years of Church history, the Church Fathers, and the rest—you will experience a "holy shock and a glorious amazement" to find that that Church, the very Church you might have been battling to save people from, is the very Church that Christ established on earth 2,000 years ago.

"Holy shock" are the only words to describe what went through me at that instant.

"Oh no." I thought, and that sense of horror returned. "Don't tell me there's any truth to this thing."

I stood paralyzed and I knew, in that instant of time, that if I did not look into the claims of the Catholic Church, I'd be turning from God.

After two years with the Friends church, I moved to New York to immerse myself in study full-time. I began by reading every

Protestant work against the Catholic Church that I could find, in the hope of being rescued from ever becoming Catholic. But in short order, I was utterly alone. It became obvious all too soon that Protestant writers were not fighting the Catholic Church, but rather what they *thought* the Catholic Church taught.

I left no stone unturned: Scripture, Tradition, the papacy, apostolic succession, the communion of saints, purgatory, every issue concerning Mary, the sacramental nature of the Church, the Mass, and above all, the Eucharist. As I studied history, the Fathers, the councils, the understanding of the faith through the writings of popes, bishops, theologians, and saints, my world began to change. I began to discover a design for God's Church on earth more beautiful, more majestic, more *whole* than anything I could have fathomed. And I discovered in time that the differences between Catholicism and Protestantism are not doctrinal only, but constitute a whole way of seeing.

The agony of my heart turned to longing for the intense beauty of what I had come to believe was true. A four-and-a-half-year journey and eighteen years of Evangelical Protestantism had come to an end.

At the Easter Vigil of 1995, I once again visited a Catholic church. And as I walked up the front steps and through the entrance, I again held my breath. But this time, I dipped my fingers in the holy water font and crossed myself in thanksgiving and submission to the God who gave himself for me. And as I walked down the central aisle, I stopped before entering the pew and went on my knees before the Tabernacle in which that God dwelt—the God of Abraham, who not only became Man but also became our Food.

During Mass, the readings from Scripture were very familiar to me. But, amazingly, so were the prayers:

> Blessed are you, Lord, God of all creation. Through your goodness we have this bread to offer, which earth has given and human hands have made. It will become the bread of life.

Could it be? I thought back to *Shabbos*, to the Sabbath prayers of our Jewish home:

*Baruch ata Adonai Elohenu Melech ha Olam hamotzi lechem min ha'aretz.*
(Blessed art Thou, O Lord, our God, King of the Universe, who
brings forth bread from the earth.)

"I came," Jesus said, "not to abolish, but to fulfill." Here was the
living Bread to which every lamb and every grain of manna
pointed. A mere symbol would not be the fulfillment of such Old
Testament types. Christ alone was the one to which every sign
pointed. The Eucharist was not symbolic: It was Christ, truly him.

And I thought about my Jewish relatives still living in Brooklyn
and about one particular family who still, to that day, would not
allow me in their home because I'd become a Christian and there-
by, to their way of thinking, had betrayed our people. My cousin
from that family had said to me one day, "I know a woman just like
you. She was also a 'Jew for Jesus,' but she went *all* the way and
became Catholic."

How did my cousin know? How did he know that to become
Catholic was to go "all the way," to be as fully Christian as a
person can get?

As I was received into the Catholic Church that night, the
Jewish Messiah—body and blood, soul and divinity—was placed
on my tongue. Oh, how could it be? What once seemed like
insanity and utterly unthinkable had become to me the measure
of the "breadth and length and height and depth" of his fathomless
love and condescension "for us men and for our salvation." O
glorious mystery of the unapproachable God who became our
Food. I sobbed uncontrollably at having at last come home—all
the way home.

I imagine that my parents were rejoicing in heaven that night,
just as David, Susan, and I had rejoiced when they had been
baptized some years earlier in a Baptist church in upstate New
York (but that's another story!). Susan is now a local missions
coordinator with the Missouri Synod Lutheran Church in Ann
Arbor, Michigan; David is president of the Association of Hebrew
Catholics in Mt. Upton, New York; and I am a staff apologist with

Catholic Answers, publisher of *This Rock*, that Catholic apologetics magazine that began my journey from my Evangelical Christian faith to its fullness in the whole Christ.

O the depth of the riches and wisdom and knowledge of God!
How unsearchable are his judgments and how inscrutable his ways!
... For from him and through him and to him are all things.
To him be glory for ever. Amen. (Rom. 11:33, 36).

*Baruch haba b'Shem Adonai!* Blessed is he who comes in the name of the Lord!